ROYAL CANADA

ROYAL CANADA

TREVOR HALL

B. Mitchell

DEDICATION

To many North American friends and royalty enthusiasts, in particular: the Dean family of Brantford, Ont. and the Dumbrille family of Maitland, Ont., who have enjoyed being on the royal route; Mrs Christopher Barnes of Bothell, Washington State, who wishes she were a little closer; and Mrs Mary Wilson of Mesquite, Texas, who follows avidly from a great distance.

ACKNOWLEDGEMENTS

The Author and Publishers wish to express their gratitude to Her Majesty the Queen for her gracious permission to reproduce photographs from The Royal Collection; to Her Royal Highness The Princess Margaret, Countess of Snowdon for the loan of photographs from her personal albums; to Her Royal Highness Princess Alexandra for making available photographs from her collection; to the Earl and Countess of Harewood for allowing a wide selection of photographs from the albums formerly owned by Her Royal Highness Princess Mary, the Princess Royal, to be used in this book; and to Lady May Abel Smith for kindly lending books of photographs assembled by her late mother, Her Royal Highness Princess Alice, Countess of Athlone.

The Author and Publishers also wish to thank the following in connection with their assistance in the preparation of this book: Miss Frances Dimond, M.V.O., Curator of the Royal Photograph Collection at Windsor Castle; the Hon. Mrs Jane Roberts, Curator of the Print Room, Royal Library, Windsor Castle; the Earl of Napier and Ettrick, C.V.O., Private Secretary to Her Royal Highness The Princess Margaret; Lieutenant Commander Sir Richard Buckley, R.N., former Private Secretary to Their Royal Highnesses the Duke and Duchess of Kent; Miss Mona Mitchell, C.V.O., Private Secretary to Her Royal Highness Princess Alexandra; Miss Sally Cox, former Personal Secretary to Their Royal Highnesses Prince and Princess Michael of Kent; Alistair Campbell of Airds, yr., Unicorn Pursuivant, at Inverary Castle, the seat of the Duke of Argyll; the staff of Public Archives, Canada; and Mr John Beaton, Manager, Library Services and his colleagues at Canapress Photo Service; Toronto.

PICTURE CREDITS

The following photographs are reproduced by gracious permission of Her Majesty The Queen: Pages 11 (bottom), 12 (top and centre), 13 (bottom), 20 (top left and top right), 22 (top right), 23 (top right and bottom), 24 (top and centre), 26, 27 (top), 29, 38 (bottom), 41.
Loaned by HRH The Princess Margaret: Pages 104 (bottom left), 112 (top left and top right).
Loaned by HRH Princess Alexandra: Pages 110 (top and bottom right), 111 (bottom), 126.
Loaned by the Earl of Harewood: Pages 98 (bottom left and bottom right), 99-101, 108 (top right, centre left, centre right and bottom).
Loaned by Lady May Abel Smith: Pages 42 (top right, bottom left and bottom right), 44, 45, 46 (top right and bottom), 47.
From the files of Central Press, Fox Photos and Keystone Press: Pages 31 (top), 35 (bottom right), 37 (bottom), 39 (top and bottom right), 40 (top left and lower left), 42 (top left and centre), 43, 46 (top left), 48, 50 (top left, top right and bottom), 51-65, 66 (top), 67, 70 (bottom left), 73 (bottom), 76, 78, 79, 92, 94-97, 98 (top, centre left and centre right), 99, 102, 103, 104 (top and bottom right), 105-107, 108 (top left), 109 (top), 110 (bottom left), 111 (top).
Canapress: Pages 66 (bottom), 68, 69, 70 (top, centre and bottom right), 71, 72, 73 (top left and top right), 74, 75, 80-91, 109 (centre and bottom), 112 (bottom), 113-123.
Rex Features: Page 146-168.
Colour Library Books: Pages 124, 127-145.
All other photographs National Archives of Canada, reference numbers as indicated.

Edited by Joanna Keywood and Edward Doling
Designed by Clive Dorman
Director of Production: Gerald Hughes
Director of Publishing: David Gibbon

CLB 2185
© 1989 Archive Publishing
A division of Colour Library Books Ltd., Godalming, Surrey, England
Printed and bound in Italy by New Interlitho
All rights reserved
ISBN 0 88665 504 8

CONTENTS

INTRODUCTION

Now will it best avail your majesty
To cross the seas, and to be crown'd in France.
The presence of a king engenders love
Amongst his subjects and his loyal friends
As it disanimates his enemies.
(Shakespeare; Henry VI, Part I: III, ii.)

In his very early twenties, Prince Charles wrote a short foreword to John Brooke's sympathetically analytical biography of George III. Both the book and its foreword were designed to turn public opinion away from the long-held view that the king said to be responsible for, amongst other things, losing a substantial chunk of the North American colonies was bad as well as mad and, indeed, that the madness was all part and parcel of the badness.

Part of Prince Charles' argument was that the former colonies were lost because George III was almost totally in America. It's a plausible theory: nothing is easier to imagine than the colonies' image of a sort of malevolent spider-figure webbed in a far-off land, issuing diktats to suit his own cause regardless of the inconvenience, stagnation or suffering they may have occasioned to a subject population. What Prince Charles then goes on to suggest is that, had the King been in a position to visit his American people - had, in fact, the concept of a royal tour been devised and developed back in the 1770's - the chances of the colonies' being forcibly surrendered would have been considerably more remote.

Here, he doubtless has a point. Equally doubtless, it is a point based on his own experiences, even at the age of 24, as a seasoned royal visitor to many far-flung regions of the world. And it is a theory that would find support in the experience of every member of his family who have, in their own right or on behalf of their sovereign, undertaken royal tours abroad. For who, even among those who might consider that the American colonies would have been lost in any event, would not wonder whether, in the much more cataclysmic two centuries that followed, Canada might not also have been tempted into republicanism but for the advent of the royal visit and its development into something of a Canadian institution?

It must, of course, be at the same time be admitted that the difference between American republicanism and Canadian loyalties to the Crown has not depended solely, or even largely, upon the frequency of royal visits to one or other country. There is such a thing as national character and emotional need, and on the whole, it seems to be the case that emotionally, the Canadians need a monarchy, even though pragmatically - as in Britain - the political and socio-economic system could work perfectly well without one. There would be no or negligible loss of national momentum if the monarchy ceased to function in Canada - after all, scores of other countries have, this century, done well enough under a presidential system. But the ties of tradition, ceremonial, personalities and even sentimentality still bind the Crown to its Canadian subjects in a way and to an extent rarely reflected in other civilisations.

Much of this stems from history itself. Some early pioneers were British, or laid claim to parts of Canada in the name of the British Crown. Later, it was the Loyalists who, in the course of the American Revolution and through to the War of 1812, fled across the border to establish, maintain and guard a whole string of fortress settlements along the St Lawrence, and did so because they preferred, for whatever reason, to owe allegiance to the King of England. The 1830's saw an unprecedented flood of British immigration into Canada which, though it might have been born of disillusion with and resentment of life in the Mother Country, was nevertheless accompanied by a perverse nostalgia and, in due time, a deeper affection for it. And once that stage of Canada's development was complete, the process of organizing and undertaking royal visits began to consolidate and nurse these sometimes tenuous strands of allegiance to Britain and to the institutions, including the monarchy, by which she was represented.

As will be revealed in the narrative of this book, the British were quick to seize upon the benefits that these strengthened links would bring. Prince Albert, with his usual impeccable foresight, spotted the potential first and worked hard to convince others of the desirability of sending the Prince of Wales to Canada in 1860. For his part, the royal traveller spent twelve days learning about Canada during the voyage, so that he was in a position to impress his hosts when he finally arrived. In the same way, and sixty years later, another Prince of Wales was to spend much of his time making the right impression, not only by being himself, but also by making the right noises, effectively flattering those he met until he had persuaded them that it was as good for them to have him there as it was for him to be there.

The charm has been worked gently over the succeeding decades. Just as the future Edward VIII insisted that he came to Canada as a Canadian - he wrote back to his father, 'I'm rubbing it in, that although not actually Canadian-born, I'm Canadian-born in spirit, and come over here as such, and not as a stranger - and that goes down well' - so other members of the Royal Family have assumed a Canadian identity. The Queen Mother once said, for instance, 'When I'm in Canada, I'm a Canadian', and has spoken quite recently of having 'lost my heart to Canada and Canadians.' Prince Andrew has described Canada as his second home. And the Queen herself has frequently emphasized her role as Queen of Canada when she has been on Canadian, or even American, soil.

These are typical instances, not merely of the need to be polite and appreciative of a host's attentions, but also of the Royal Family's awareness, particularly in recent years, of how important this kind of behaviour is to the very existence of the Crown in Canada. For behind the serene façade that royal activity often displays, lies an active concern for the way in which the Crown is perceived. One of the best examples of this concern is also one of the first, and it arose during the Queen's Australian Tour of 1963. It was conceived and planned much as any other Commonwealth visit, with the Queen journeying everywhere in majestic isolation - either enclosed in an aircraft, a lone figure on the deck of a far-off ship, or gliding by in a gleaming limousine. The Australians, who had seen it all before and lapped it up in 1954, were now unimpressed by a mere repeat performance nine years later, and the thinness of the crowds proved it. The Queen's advisers immediately got to work to determine the reasons for this unexpected indifference, and by the time the Queen went back to the Antipodes in 1970, the magic formula of the walkabout had been evolved. It meant the Queen had to step down from the somewhat heroic pedestal that she had been accustomed to assume, and to press the flesh, but it was considered a price well worth paying to keep the Crown secure in popular affections. In addition, the pace of royal visits to Australasia was stepped up to maintain the profile in an age when image has increasingly called the tune.

Such considerations were less applicable to Canada, since major royal visits had always been sustained at a much more frequent level since the very beginning of the Queen's reign. But the lessons learned in Australia have been applied to visits to Canada, and the gradual but noticeable progression of relaxed informality which has characterised each succeeding visit, particularly where younger members of the Royal Family are concerned, is the well-received fruit of a continuing royal awareness of popular demands and reactions.

Although it can be shown that, in general, the Canadians have maintained a healthy respect, a genuine love, and indeed a continuing fascination for the Royal Family for a very long time, any statement to that effect must of course be something of a generalisation. It generalises place, since it is patent to all that the pockets of greatest continuing loyalty to the Crown are in the Maritime Provinces, the old Loyalist strongholds, and British Columbia. It generalises people, because with the best will in the world one cannot safely assume that more than a minority of Francophones feel a substantial degree of natural loyalty, nor can the same be expected of the millions who have immigrated from Eastern Europe, South America and Asia in the last few decades, and whose own ties with their respective homelands and ethnic customs must be stronger influences on their lives. And, of course, it generalises time, for it has certainly not always been true that Canada as a political unit has allowed its habitual deference to the Crown to interfere with its political development and aspirations. Conversely, it is the case that various critical stages in Canada's political development - especially where the interests of English and French Canadians were in conflict - have placed a degree of strain on relations with the Crown.

One issue discussed at the 1897 Colonial Conference, for instance, was whether Canada, whose contacts with the outside world were administered almost entirely through the British Foreign Office, would be expected to support Britain with money and men in any conflict involving the Mother Country. Prime Minister Laurier maintained an inscrutable silence at that conference, and subsequently held that each case should be decided on its merits. When the matter was raised in Canada on the outbreak of the Anglo-Boer War in 1899, the English Canadians were for supporting Britain, the French against. Fortunately for Britain, a compromise was reached whereby Canadian troops would be sent to South Africa as volunteers only, serving under British command and paid from British funds. The Duke of York, visiting Canada towards the end of that war, made a special point of expressing Britain's gratitude for this facility, and to that extent his tour was used as a political convenience on behalf of the British government.

An even more pointed use of the Royal Family for political purposes developed in 1939, when the King and Queen undertook their six-week tour as Europe began to prepare itself for possible war. Of course, no such admission that the tour was largely a recruiting drive was forthcoming from the British or Canadian authorities, particularly when that purpose was ferociously criticised by Dr Norman Bethune, one of Canada's greatest medical pioneers. But there was no doubting the ulterior motive, especially as the very same considerations made it imperative that the King and Queen should also encompass a personal visit to President Roosevelt within their North American itinerary. In more recent times, the political volatility of Quebec has meant that the present Queen and most members of her family gave the city and province a wide berth for almost a quarter of a century - partly, and in the earlier stages of turmoil, for security reasons, and partly in the interests of political diplomacy, until the separatist issue was resolved to most people's satisfaction.

For all that events have influenced Canadians' views of their links with Britain, it must be said that they have rarely affected, to any great detriment, their relations with the monarchy, the monarch, and the various members of the Royal Family personally. Of course, the occasion of one or other royal visits has been used as the catalyst for protest - be it Suez, Northern Ireland or Quebec - and not every royal visitor has been equally welcome: witness various newspaper criticisms of Prince Philip's speeches, Prince Andrew's comments and Princess Margaret's private life. But generally, Canadians have proved welcoming, consistent and imaginative hosts, keen to show their royalty the best of their land and to involve it in the most spectacular of their festivals. In return, the royal guests have offered and re-offered themselves to the service of Canada and her people in a way which is not merely declamatory, but graphically illustrated by the vast number of visits that have taken place during the present reign.

The *quid pro quo* was neatly summed up by the Queen at the end of her 1984 tour, when she said: 'The crowds of people of all ethnic origins and denominations who gave me such a warm welcome and who came to the celebratory events, demonstrated that the Crown still has a real value, and I shall continue to fulfil my duties as Queen of Canada to the best of my abilities and in the interests of all Canadians.' It is the sort of promise which the Queen has renewed time and again during her reign, and to which Canadians have been reacting with powerful appreciation. It is, of course, also a promise to which Canadians will hold their sovereign and the increasing number of family members who come to her shores and visit her fascinating interior and adventurous people. It has long been a source of pride among the people of Canada that they have given of their best for every visiting royal, in spite of the doubtful beginnings when the future King William IV ventured reluctantly to British North America with the Royal Navy. The welcoming tradition, now in its third century, becomes more effusive, more creative and more loyal the more it is tested, and the personal reasons for it are probably as manifold and various as the number of loyal Canadians.

For the Queen, in particular - a woman of natural reserve and not given to effusive expression - each arrival in Canada is a welcome into the bosom of an overseas family; each departure something of a domestic wrench even after the days, sometimes weeks, of unveiling plaques, planting trees, making speeches, shaking hands, receiving bouquets and the endless, endless travelling which makes privileged routine no less routine for being privileged. The strength of that familial pull is constantly expressed by the Queen's insistence that she is, after all, Queen of a family called Canada. But now and again, she lets slip a more personal comment - much more telling because of its comparative rarity and spontaneity - as she did on leaving west-coast America for British Columbia in March 1983: 'We're going home to Canada tomorrow!'

CHAPTER ONE

COLONY TO CONFEDERATION

MISERY AND MISTRESSES: AN UNPROMISING PRELUDE

The standing joke on the subject of advancing years is that the older you get, the less inclined you are to celebrate your birthday. This may be so with individuals, who rarely like to be reminded of the passage of time and the onset of middle or old age. But there is nothing a nation enjoys more than an anniversary, and Canadians are past masters in the art of celebrating the various birthdays that mark their country's historic progress from its days as a colony to its present status as a fully-fledged independent political entity. As a nation, Canadians are proud of an inheritance won in the teeth of struggle and adversity, developed in an ethnic tolerance of a degree that most multi-racial countries of the world would give their eye-teeth to achieve, and kept alive by its own frequent celebration. In the last hundred years or so, therefore, no national centenary, bicentenary, sesquicentenary, golden or diamond jubilee, or any other major anniversary of any constitutional development, or provincial, town or city status has gone uncelebrated in the big, broad, Canadian manner.

It may be argued that, in this respect, Canadians are much like any other people who pride themselves on their achievements. But where Canadians are very much the exception is in the fervour with which they love to involve the Royal Family in those celebrations. The British tend to take the royals very much for granted - an understandable reaction to a secure, virtually unbroken, though constantly changing relationship between Crown and people which has lasted for over ten centuries. Australia and New Zealand, to be sure, keep their partnership with the Royal Family warm, and almost a score of other Commonwealth nations, who since independence have retained the Queen as their Head of State, find the circumstance comfortable and acceptable. But no nation, within or outwith the Commonwealth, can boast such a high level of royal-hosting than Canada. Nearly eighty royal visits of varying lengths in the last thirty-five years is no mean feat when you realise that the public demands on your guests from all corners of the world are such that they are obliged to turn away a dozen invitations for every one they accept.

For all that, it was always unlikely that, come the high summer of 1986, Canadians would feel at all moved to celebrate a quite historic royal anniversary - the bicentennial of the first royal visit to their shores. This may have been because it was not a visit in the sense we recognise today.

Alternatively, and much more feasibly, it might have been because the episode was distinguished by a general indifference on the part of the colonials and by decidedly bad grace on the part of the royal visitor. He was Prince William, the third son of George III, the king to whom history often rather unfairly attributes the entire blame for the loss of the American colonies just a few years earlier. Prince William, then serving in the Royal Navy, had good reason to be less than bowled over by the prospect of a sojourn in what was then fondly known as British North America, for it amounted to little more than an involuntary exile. His father, determined to regulate the affairs of his errant sons with greater success as a parent than he had been able to achieve as a constitutional monarch over the Americans, had recently learned of yet another in a long line of William's amorous escapades, and had insisted that the need to avoid complications and inconvenient personal obligations was best served by a long spell overseas. The Prince jibbed mightily at the prospect, but found few supporters within his family in his struggle to change his father's mind. Eventually he succumbed to the inevitable, though only after a long and bitter wrangle from which he secured the naval promotion he had for many unsuccessful months been seeking through other channels.

It was thus as a post-captain in charge of the 28-gun frigate *Pegasus* that William arrived in July 1786 off the coast of Newfoundland. Any self-satisfaction he may have felt at the accomplishment of his first voyage in his new command, however, was quickly extinguished by his first view of St John's. 'Truly deplorable,' he grumbled. 'A small brushwood for the first five hundred yards inshore, and then a most dreadful, inhospitable and barren country.' It was indeed an inauspicious start to what was to become two centuries of largely happy and certainly colourful, eventful and festive royal visits to a country that rapidly developed from colonial to dominion status and thence to eventual statehood. But the discontented Prince William was soon to discover that his troubles were in fact only just beginning. At Placentia Bay he had to quell a riot involving a horde of drunken Irish fishermen, and shortly afterwards was bemoaning the unexpectedly early severity of the weather which by the end of August had left thick ice covering the puddles in the main streets. Nova Scotia he found decidedly more tolerable. It was certainly considerably warmer there, and very much livelier, but what especially attracted this lustiest of the King's many sons was its inexhaustible supply of women 'of the most obliging kind'. Within days of his identity becoming widely known, his status as a prince of the blood royal left him spoilt for choice, and he quickly discovered that the pleasures of the flesh - always enjoyable even in the inhibiting circumstances of naval life closer to home - were positively enthralling in the relative freedom in which he now found himself.

His time in Nova Scotia proved something of a high point in his Canadian experiences. It was here that he discovered a fondness for Frances Wentworth, the wife of the man appointed as Surveyor of the King's Woods in North America. Though the King himself seems to have known nothing of this liaison, fate proved an efficient long-stop. Before long, the Prince was instructed by the Admiralty back in London to proceed to the West Indies on a naval tour which kept him away from Canada for a full year. When, at the end of that time, his ship berthed at Quebec, he was as different again from the dashing young buck who had captivated the females of Halifax. He was carried ashore with a high-running tropical fever which debilitated him and sent him into a succession of delirious ravings. He was financially crippled as well, with debts which he had allowed to accumulate freely, in spite assurances from his father that he would not be baled out. Renewed appeals for cash went unheeded, even though he attempted to please the King by presenting an attractive, if somewhat overdone, picture of Canada and a less than handsome picture of the Canadians. 'The ground is rich,' he wrote in the Autumn of 1787, 'and if the industrious Englishman tilled it instead of the lazy Canadian, it would be inestimable.' Small wonder that, as King William IV, he found little difficulty, and suffered no stab of conscience, in opposing the onset of electoral democracy in Lower Canada in 1835.

In the meantime, William's younger brother Edward, later Duke of Kent, spent what might be described as a rather more fruitful time in Canada. In 1791, he sailed for Quebec to take command of a regiment of Fusiliers, and within the year had formed a serious, though extra-marital, relationship with Mme Julie de St Laurent, the lady who became his mistress and remained faithful to him in that capacity until the prospect of fathering a future British sovereign eventually persuaded him, at the age of fifty, into a respectable marriage. But to Canadians, in those last years of the eighteenth century, Prince and mistress were as good as husband and wife. Mme de Laurent enjoyed a wide social coterie in Quebec, and the Prince leased a sizeable villa on Bedford Basin which became the base for a whirling social life full of parties, recitals and concerts. The story goes that the pair were

NATIONAL ARCHIVES OF CANADA/C-3689

NATIONAL ARCHIVES OF CANADA/C-1271

NATIONAL ARCHIVES OF CANADA/PA-147523

TOP: The Prince of Wales (6th from left) visits Point View, Niagara; ABOVE at Government House, Charlottetown; and LEFT with his suite, the Prince standing 5th from right. OPPOSITE PAGE: exercise in excision: top photograph shows the Prince's party including (l. to r.) Sir Edmund Head, Captain Grey (equerry), the Duke of Newcastle, General Bruce. The centre photo, montaged against a more attractive background, expunges the equerry. BOTTOM: the Prince's youngest brother, Prince Arthur, in military winter costume during his year's stay in Canada, January 1870.

so strongly accepted as a married couple that they acted as joint godparents at the baptism of the son of one of their friends. Within a short time, however, they were themselves in the business of procreation, and Prince Edward had fathered at least two children by his paramour - one known as Robert Wood, the other as William Goodall Green - by the time he left Quebec for Halifax.

Here he became Commander-in-Chief of the troops in Nova Scotia and New Brunswick, and had a new citadel built for military defence, together with new signalling systems, batteries and towers. Mme de St Laurent accompanied him to his new posting, but the children - a clear embarrassment to public life on the move - were left behind to be brought up by paid supervisors. It seems today something of a tragedy of hypocrisy that, in the fullness of time, an island in the Gulf of St Lawrence was, with great public flourish, named after him, while the children of his private pleasures were not. Despite their father's elevation in 1799 to Commander of all the King's North American forces, and his well-recognised achievement in establishing good relations with the French–speaking communities who were still smarting under the British régime, the two illegitimate sons drifted into comparative anonymity and social limbo, although Robert Wood did make something of a name for himself in the lumber industry in Lower Canada. It was even sadder, in the longer term, that Prince Edward's final departure from Canada, forced upon him in 1800 (after an injury following a fall from his horse had obliged him to return to England for treatment in 1798), marked the temporary discontinuance of any royal presence in the colony until well past the middle of the nineteenth century, though by then the auguries were much more positive and benign.

TEENAGE TOURIST: A SPECTACULAR VICTORIAN EXPERIMENT

The long, tedious and expensive reigns of the royal geriatrics - George III, George IV and William IV - had passed, and the era of Prince Edward's only daughter, the dutiful and conscientious Queen Victoria, whom Canadians still hold in great respect bordering on awe, was a time for creating precedents and exploring new avenues of relationship between the Crown and the instruments of the growing imperial heritage. It is Victoria's eldest son - Albert Edward, Prince of Wales - to whom the pioneering spirit of becoming a royal ambassador of Empire is credited, and it was Canada that secured the honour of his first official foreign tour in 1860. His mother had in the first instance been surprisingly reluctant with her permission. She had refused an invitation to visit Canada herself, for fear of the dangers and fatigue of a long voyage, and it was only in recognition of Canadian loyalty in sending a regiment to join the British troops in the Crimea in 1856 that she eventually felt impelled to offer her son and heir as her delegate.

Then it was the turn of the British politicians to become sceptical of the value of the Prince's prospective journey, and even ministers in the Colonial Office became infected with the general lack of zeal. But the Prince's father, Prince Albert, not to mention the editor of *The Times*, was convinced that there was mileage to be made from 'the useful co-operation of the Royal Family in the civilisation which England developed and advanced.' For the Prince of Wales himself, the idea offered a liberating alternative to a dull and seemingly endless diet of filial duty and academic study, and he seized the opportunity for exploiting the wider horizons with glee.

He may not have found the outward voyage much to his

liking, over-full as it was of studying maps and memorising constitutional details, but once in Canada, he never looked back. After a twelve-day voyage from Plymouth, the Prince arrived at St John's, Newfoundland, then a mere fishing station. Despite pouring rain, which was to dog much of his time there, everything came alive with his entry into Halifax at the end of July, where celebrations waxed so comprehensive that stores closed down for two days and even newspapers failed to appear. From then until the end of his two-month stay, his schedule was packed with processions, levees, banquets, audiences and interminable addresses of welcome. He sent frequent letters - dutifully factual, though rarely enthusiastic - back home, enclosing with one of them a piece of sweet briar taken from the derelict remains of the Duke of Kent's Lodge, which, as we have seen, his grandfather had occupied over sixty years before.

From Nova Scotia he travelled, in that same grandfather's footsteps, to New Brunswick, spending two days in Saint John, travelling by boat across Grand Bay and along the Saint John River to Fredericton. It was here that he learned by telegram of the birth of his first niece, Princess Charlotte of Prussia, the sister of the future Kaiser Wilhelm II.

Meanwhile, the Duke of Newcastle, charged by Queen Victoria and Prince Albert to keep a fatherly eye on their wayward son's doings, was able to report how impressed the Canadians were by the Prince's manner - 'frank and friendly, without any mixture of assumed study to gain popularity by over-civility.' At Quebec, he was properly polite with Roman Catholic church leaders, and they responded in kind. He was duly impressed by Montreal's new Victoria Bridge which he was invited to open officially, correctly solemn on opening the new Parliament Buildings in Ottawa, and his father, much of whose life's work was devoted to re-organising and making efficient the network of royal farms from Osborne to Balmoral, would have been proud of the interest he showed in the exhibition of farm produce he attended at Toronto. Clearly his forte was his personality, which never prospered

ABOVE: Prince Arthur, arms folded, with his group (including five Indians) on their return from a hunt early in 1870, untying game and lighting a camp fire.
RIGHT: the Prince in walking dress: a studio portrait taken in January 1870. BELOW: Prince Arthur at Lord and Lady Lisgar's home, Belmere, during his visit to Lake Memphremagog in Quebec Province that year.

better than with the easy going Canadians and particularly at the many all-night balls staged in his honour.

At the Mayor's Ball in Quebec, for instance, he was on the dance-floor throughout the night, taking part in every one of the twenty-two dances. At Montreal, too, he refused to sit out a single dance in that famous and extravagant ballroom, with its fountains running with claret and champagne, and its superb gardens with their artificial lakes splendidly illuminated. Every woman fell for his charm and, like his great-uncle Prince William, he did nothing to discourage their blind and sometimes openly sensual devotion. At a ball in Hamilton he exchanged mischievous whispers with them with such abandon that *The New York Herald* was convinced that 'he looks as if he might have a very susceptible nature, and has already yielded to several twinges in the region of his midriff.'

News of his affable behaviour preceded him everywhere, and even affected the occasionally delicate politics of the times. To his triumphant entry into Quebec was imputed an almost miraculous cooling of hostility between French and British sympathisers. At Kingston, the ultra-Protestant and pro-British Orangemen, faced with the Prince's refusal to land unless they removed their Orange arches and played down the sectarian tenor of their prospective welcome, defied his ultimatum by drafting a drunken resolution inviting him 'to land and be decorated with Orange orders, or to go to hell and take his flunkeys with him.' Then, two days later, they turned up at Toronto and, full of apologies, a delegation of hitherto confident, grown and hardy men tearfully begged the forgiveness of this 18-year-old boy.

Elsewhere, that same sense of fun for which his own grandson, the future King Edward VIII, was to become equally well, if not better, known captivated the Canadians. He took a ride on a timber slide at Hull - the first of many such royal thrills - and shot the St Lawrence rapids on a raft. Then, having watched Charles Blondin's walk across Niagara Falls on a tightrope - a feat rather pompously described by *The Times* in London as 'fitting the performer for the highest place in a lunatic asylum' - he even volunteered to be taken across the Falls in Blondin's wheelbarrow, until Lord Newcastle prevented him. To repay his enthusiasm and spontaneity, his hosts could not do enough for him. The Falls were illuminated in his honour, Indian tribes emerged everywhere to greet him, he rode in State under innumerable triumphal arches bedecked with flowers and bearing messages of unmistakeable loyalty, and his comings and goings spawned a rash of advertisements which used his name to peddle everything from umbrellas to cans of baked beans.

It was a hugely successful personal visit, though Lord Newcastle perceived a longer-term benefit. He told Queen Victoria that the future would demonstrate 'the good that has been done. The attachment to the Crown of England has been greatly cemented, and other nations have learned how useless it will be in the case of war to tamper with the allegiance of the North American province.' None of these high-minded thoughts were of much consolation to the Prince of Wales, however, as he voyaged back to England in HMS *Hero*, the same screw-driven battleship that had brought him to Canada. The journey was a true November nightmare,

TOP: an ornate heroic sculpture presented to the Marquess of Lorne on his taking office in 1878.
CENTRE: Princess Louise, Lord Lorne's wife, and Queen Victoria's highly artistic daughter – a portrait taken during her husband's Governor-Generalship.
LEFT: the visit of Prince Leopold, brother of Princess Louise, to Government House in 1880: the Princess stands behind her brother.

with frighteningly high seas and such constantly adverse winds and foul weather that the ship's speed was severely reduced. It took the Prince twenty-six long and uncomfortable days to reach home, over twice as long as the outward journey.

In those circumstances, it was a wonder that his brother, Prince Alfred, followed suit the next year. But he had already decided to make the Royal Navy his career, and every aspiring naval officer worth his salt was expected to be more than a match for the hazards of sea voyages. Prince Alfred, who spent a total of over five weeks in the Maritime Provinces before moving onto Quebec City, disembarked at Saint John, New Brunswick in torrential midnight rain, to a ceremonial greeting from over six hundred uniformed firemen carrying torches. His presence in the Maritimes, perhaps in the wake of his elder brother's visit, brought out the worst of the social climbing instincts of what one local newspaper termed 'certain would-be exclusives who endeavoured to monopolise the Prince and prevented the common people from getting a sight of him.' Prince Alfred, however, and in spite of his young years - he was only sixteen at the time - decided to embark upon his own private itinerary in Saint John, and was soon seen 'walking and driving about the city to the various points of interest', and emulating the essentially casual attitude that had characterised his brother's leisure time in Canada and so charmed the Canadians.

And so, it is possible to detect something of a precedent in connection with this new phenomenon, in which the British sovereign despatched members of her immediate family to parts of her growing Empire. It became a regular feature of colonial life, with various sons, daughters, and eventually grandchildren travelling to Australasia, South Africa, Egypt and the Indian sub-continent. Indeed, as travel became safer and the adventuring spirit of the British grew, the royal mission to individual countries newly brought under the imperial wing became *de rigueur*. But it was those pioneering set tours of an emergent Canada that blazed the trail. And conversely, it was the warmth with which Canadians received the royal ambassadors that began to convince the British authorities that a more permanent royal presence in the country might not be such a bad thing.

LORNE'S CANADA: A TRUE AFFINITY

Thus, the undoubted success of the Prince of Wales' lengthy and hectic tour effectively began the rewarding, personal association between the Royal Family and the Canadian people that has reflected and warmed the constitutional development between Canada and Britain in the last century and a quarter. By the middle of the 1870's, when the notion of Empire became an open reality with the proclamation of Queen Victoria as Empress of India, the Canadians were of a mind to merge their personal and constitutional links with the Crown by accepting the sovereign's appointment of members of the Royal Family as the country's Governors-General. That began a spell of almost seventy years during which the colony - a Confederation after 1867 - enjoyed the reality or the prospect of having royalty presiding over its increasingly independent political, social and economic life.

The first and, for a long time, only such experience came with the appointment of the Marquess of Lorne, son of the Scottish Duke of Argyll, as Canada's Governor-General in 1878. Seven years earlier he had married the Queen's fourth daughter, Princess Louise, thus setting a latter-day precedent for the marriage of British royalty into classes of inferior social rank. Both partners were by temperament and their mutual love of the arts unquestionably suited to each other, and in those early days the promise of their own microcosm of royal life in Canada seemed a logical and propitious turn of fate.

At first, the reality seemed less so. The royal couple arrived off Halifax in the most hostile of weather, and tempestuous waters kept their ship, the *Sarmatian*, heaving helplessly out at sea for over twenty-four alarming hours, while they looked imploringly from the deck toward land through the driving rain. The Princess' elder brother, Alfred - by then he had married and been created Duke of Edinburgh - had reached Nova Scotia some days earlier, and when the weather eventually calmed, was able to escort her and her husband to shore for a private stay on *terra firma*, before the national welcome two days later saw them come ashore again, officially, to the crackle of gun-salutes, the flutter of flags, the bray of brass bands and the presentation of gifts. One working-class politician actually assured the Marquess of Lorne that his coming had excited the whole of Canada, down to every labourer and newsboy, while local newspapers began as they meant to continue, and gave minutely detailed accounts of each ceremony and the dress and demeanour of the royal couple.

By today's standards, the reporting of this, and of the subsequent activities of the Princess and her husband, was cloying and pompous - so much so that it tended to be out of step with the very character of their life-style. The Lornes took quickly to skating - they hosted numerous skating parties at Rideau Hall - sightseeing and even shopping expeditions, during which the Princess in particular mingled freely with the crowds. Before long, they had immersed themselves in the incipient Canadian culture, and had comprehended the root of the traditional hostility of the Indians toward the white settlers. The Marquess and his wife became engrossed in the country's natural life, an interest reflected by their small personal collection of two moose, an aviary of local birds, and an Esquimaux dog that distinguished itself by its propensity to tear up every newspaper it could find. Social matters fascinated the Lornes: the Princess made a point of speaking up for the then generally unpopular notion of education for women - an essential prerequisite, she insisted, to an efficiently-run domestic system - while both she and her husband discovered to their pleasant surprise an abundance of Scottish exiles, including the grandson of one of Queen Victoria's gillies, and several expatriate friends of the Argyll family. Indeed, they remarked with some amusement that on Prince Edward Island, Gaelic was more widely spoken than English.

It was perhaps inevitable that the flush of their new experience made life for the Lornes something of a holiday. The Marquess had a large private house built on the Cascapedian River and used it as a base for canoeing and salmon-fishing expeditions for himself and his wife. It was here that Princess Louise made many of her sketches and completed several paintings of Canadian scenery and wildlife, and the relaxing surroundings and associations made the house as preferable to their official Canadian residences as Balmoral was to Buckingham Palace or Holyroodhouse for Queen Victoria.

At the same time the Lornes did not ignore the duties which had brought them to Canada. In addition to the official administrative work which kept the Marquess in Ottawa for long periods of time, there were tours to undertake, like those of Prince Edward Island and Western Ontario in the early part

ABOVE: a severely formal portrait of Princess Louise, taken in Ottawa in 1879. RIGHT: an official photograph of the Marquess of Lorne, taken in 1879 and showing him wearing the Garter and Thistle Stars and the Royal Victorian Order. BELOW: the impressive scene in the Senate Chamber as the Marquess took the Oath of Office in 1878, a ceremony watched by Princess Louise (extreme left). Lord Lorne was the 26th Governor-General since British rule, and the fourth since Confederation.

ABOVE CENTRE: a household staff group at Rideau Hall in the early 1880s, with Princess Louise standing, and Lord Lorne seated to her left. ABOVE: Lord Lorne dressed for winter, in January 1879. BELOW: the arrival in Canada of the royal couple, though a modest pair by standards of the day, set up the country's socialites admirably, and ushered in a new era of social brilliance. This photograph of a glittering ball given in 1879 in honour of the new Governor-General and his wife at the Windsor Hotel, Montreal, typifies the new social atmosphere.

NATIONAL ARCHIVES OF CANADA/PA-127314

LEFT: Princess Louise with a party of friends and staff in front of the toboggan slide at Rideau Hall, ca. 1880. BELOW: the Lornes with their eighteen-year-old nephew, Prince George of Wales, at Rideau Hall in September 1883, towards the end of Lord Lorne's tenure of office. BOTTOM: Prince Arthur of Connaught, son of the 1869-70 royal visitor, at Loretto Convent, Niagara, during his 1906 tour. OPPOSITE PAGE, TOP: Prince Arthur arrives for a reception at Regina, Sask. and BOTTOM by the Niagara River (Prince Arthur is to left of picture).

of 1879, and the 'Great Western Journey', as it became known, of 1882 - an eight-week marathon which took them across to Victoria by way of Chicago, Omaha, Nevada and San Francisco, then up the Fraser River and back to Vancouver before going south again to winter in the United States.

On this trip they suffered one of several accidents which were to bedevil Lord Lorne's five-year term as Governor-General. While he and the Princess were travelling by train through the Canadian Rockies, an axle of their engine broke. Fortunately the fault occurred during a relatively rare stretch of level track; the consequences might otherwise have been nothing less than final. One earlier mishap, in March 1880, involved another locomotive as it took them from Ottawa to Montreal. This was a 'special' train, for which the scheduled, regular Montreal-Ottawa express was to have stopped *en route*. As luck would have it, the system which was to have operated this pause in the express' progress failed when a switch jammed, and it took a quick-thinking and courageous railway operative to run up the line, waving his hands frantically at the driver of the Governor-General's train to persuade him – successfully, in events – to stop.

NATIONAL ARCHIVES OF CANADA/PA-12200

An even worse accident had befallen only two months previously when the royal couple were being drawn by horse and carriage to an official function in Ottawa. With thick ice and snow on the roads, the carriage was mounted on runners. Suddenly, one of the horses bolted, taking the others with him. The carriage was dragged along for several hundred yards, eventually crashing onto its side, before the horses were brought to a halt by a passer-by with more presence of mind than thought for his own safety. Rescuers pulled out the bedraggled occupants to find the Governor-General badly shaken, and the Princess injured and bleeding, with the lobe of one ear completely severed.

Disastrous though this was, that things could have been worse was demonstrated in July 1882 when the royal couple's yacht collided with a schooner while they were returning to Quebec after a pleasure-trip down-river. There was serious damage to the yacht, including a broken mast which, had it completed its fall uninterrupted, would almost certainly have struck and killed the Princess. As it was, the Marquess managed to pull his wife out of the way, at the same time diverting the path of the collapsing mast. The royal couple breathed again, and lived to tell the story.

NATIONAL ARCHIVES OF CANADA/PA-51521

NATIONAL ARCHIVES OF CANADA/PA-32593

NATIONAL ARCHIVES OF CANADA/C-49571

had it that the wife of the Prime Minister and Princess Louise were at daggers drawn. The story endured throughout the Marquess' entire term, with never an opportunity lost to convert the reporting of any social or official encounter between any of the parties concerned into a tale of snubs, insults and bitter recriminations. Letters, and supposed letters, on the subject went into circulation for some thirty years, and the argument about relationships between the Macdonalds and the Lornes (which in fact remained warm and cordial) never really let up until shortly before Lord Lorne's death – by then he had succeeded his father as Duke of Argyll – in 1914.

The other rumour that dogged the royal couple throughout the Governor–Generalship concerned the state of their marriage. On this subject, though much information seems to be lacking, there appears to be rather more justification for the stories of infidelity and neglect on the part of the Marquess, which resulted in a growing tendency for Princess Louise to absent herself from her husband's side. Few eyebrows were raised when, having experienced the severity of Ottawa's 1878-9 winter, the Princess decided to spend the following winter in England, but when, having returned in January 1880, she left for British shores again in July and spent the whole of the next twelve months touring Europe, the gossip began to circulate. A public statement issued on her behalf and citing her health as the cause of her continued absence from Canada failed to cut any ice, and eventually Lord Lorne himself crossed the Atlantic to see his wife. When, two months later, he left for Canada again, he travelled alone, his wife seeing him off from Liverpool with the promise that she would be back in Ottawa within four months. Only a few days late, she eventually arrived to the welcoming blast of cannon from the Heights of Abraham in June 1882, after an absence of almost two years.

But for all the drawbacks, the Marquess of Lorne's term of office was widely regarded as a successful and prestigious one, distinguished by the royal couple's interest in Canada's artistic heritage. Princess Louise (who set up her own art studio at Rideau Hall) encouraged the foundation of the Canadian Academy of Arts in 1880, presented her own painting *A View of Glen Shira, Inveraray* to Montreal's Art Gallery which she opened in 1879, donated other paintings to form the basis of what is now the National Gallery of Canada, and completed several sketchbooks with watercolours commemorating her stay in the Confederation. The Marquess, himself a well-informed art connoisseur and an accomplished author, published two books, *Memories of Scotland and Canada* and *Canadian Pictures*, which remained popular long after his term had come to an end, and a travelogue entitled *Our Railway to the Pacific*.

The Canadians were sorry in 1883 to see the Lornes leave, as in drizzling rain and thick mud they made their way to their ship, the *Sardinian*, which was to take them back to England. Lord Lorne was made an honorary grand chieftain of the Hurons, while Sir John Macdonald described him heartily as 'a right good fellow –and a good Canadian'. As for Princess Louise, the official reminders long outlived her presence in Canada, and some exist even today. Regiments, like Princess Louise's Dragoon Guards, were named after her, as was Quebec's Louise Embankment, the Rockies' Lake Louise in the heart of the then new national park near Banff, Princess Louise's British Fund and – it is sometimes overlooked – the province of Alberta, which took its name from the last of the Princess' three Christian names. '*Revenez encore*,' pleaded the banners strung across Ottawa's main roads as the royal couple took their leave. But they never did. Indeed, it was to be over a quarter of a century before a royal Governor-General set foot in Canada again.

In a sense, the physical dangers and inconveniences were as nothing compared with the pressures and controversies of official life. Lord Lorne quickly proved himself no mere rubber stamp, and became noted for his opposition to the 'spoils of office' system to which most Canadian federal and provincial politicians had tacitly succumbed. That the Marquess was very much his own man was shown within only a few weeks of his taking office, when the dismissal by the new Conservative Prime Minister, Sir John Macdonald, of Quebec's Liberal Lieutenant-Governor Letellier (who himself had dismissed the province's Conservative administration) was said to have caused an irreparable difference of opinion between the Governor-General and the Prime Minister. Predictably in an age when the Canadian press prided itself for being always on the attack, the supposed constitutional schism was widely reported to have spilled over into the protagonists' personal relationships, and before long rumour

CHAPTER TWO

THE LINKING OF ARMS

SOLEMNITY AND CELEBRATION; THE EDWARDIANS CONSOLIDATE

Bearing in mind the phenomenal success of Albert Edward, Prince of Wales' 1860 visit to Canada, it was a shame that he never returned. Even as King, he found a convenient excuse for refusing an invitation to visit the country for Quebec's tercentenary in 1908, despite an unctuous, though well-meant, plea to 'allow Canadians to express their profound admiration for those kingly virtues and truly humanitarian deeds which have earned Your Majesty the first place amongst the great sovereigns of the world.' Concealing the fact that he was a European at heart, he pleaded the necessity of being within call of England, and sent his son, the future King George V, to Canada instead. It turned out to be a happy substitution. Despite his innate conservatism and unadventuresome nature, the then Prince of Wales found himself at ease among the different cultures he encountered. He was careful to avoid patronising the understandably sensitive French Canadians, taking especial pains not to exclude mention of the French contribution to Canada's history. At Wolfe's Monument, for instance, he spoke emphatically of 'the historic battlefields of Quebec, on which two contending races won equal and imperishable glory.' And throughout the week-long visit, he pioneered the now traditional formula of speaking to the Quebecois in French as well as English.

'The Prince of Wales has taught the people of Quebec how to cheer,' wrote the Governor-General as the visit came to a close, and even the Prince himself reflected gratefully that relations between English and French Canadians had never been better. He was thrilled to be able to present a cheque for £90,000, representing Empire-wide donations for the acquisition by the Canadian people of the Quebec battlefields, as no doubt his wife was thrilled by at least one of the gifts he took back for her – a mink coat with 24-carat gold buttons, presented to him by the people of Nova Scotia.

The Prince of Wales had, as Duke of York, and with his wife, the former Princess May of Teck, already paid a major official visit to Canada in the autumn of 1901. It was part of a monumental eight-month tour of the Empire, which had been proposed as early as 1898, but delayed so that the first Australian Federal Parliament could be opened in State in mid-1901. The North American stage of the tour was also the final one but, then as now, exuberance was the hallmark of the Canadian welcome, just as the most unpleasant weather

had become almost a feature of royal arrivals there. Fog, then rain, hampered the Duke and Duchess' vessel HMS *Ophir* on its progress up the St. Lawrence, and a squally wind turned into a frightening storm as she dropped anchor at Quebec. But there were huge crowds to greet them, the blaze of bunting in harbour and streets mirrored by the overall dressing of warships - tempered though this was by the half-masted American flag in memory of the recently assassinated President McKinley. A spectacular firework display, staged that evening before an illuminated fleet, was marred when one tug's consignment of fireworks blew up prematurely, setting the whole craft instantly ablaze, and sending explosions rocketing off in all directions.

Visiting, as he was, in the middle of the Boer War, the Duke - then on his third trip to Quebec since he had visited privately as a young man during the Lorne Governor-Generalship - took care to thank the Canadians for their contribution to the war effort, deftly shielding the reality of that conflict's cost in human life behind the hope that 'the blood shed on battlefields in South Africa may, like that shed by your fathers in 1775 and 1812, weave fresh strands in the cord of brotherhood that binds together our glorious Empire'.

That sentiment grates today, so it is good - even somewhat surprising - to know that the Duke, as a young man at least, was capable of more perceptive, less hidebound reactions to events and situations. At Ottawa, he described the federation of Canada as pre-eminent among the political events of the nineteenth century. At Regina, he vividly contrasted the free, healthy and useful life of the area with the narrow and alas! too often unwholesome existence of the thousands in our great cities at home, and he repeated this theme on his return to London when, in his famous 'Wake Up, England!' speech at the Guildhall, he called for more emigration to take advantage of opportunities in the Colonies. At Calgary, he marshalled all his diplomatic tact to reply to the Alberta Indians in their own parlance, speaking of Queen Victoria as the Great Mother, of earlier years of troubles as 'days when your pipes were cold, your tents melancholy', and giving assurances that 'my Great Father the King's promises will last as long as sun shall shine and waters shall flow'.

The welcome the Indians gave him was arguably the most colourful - certainly the most unusual - of the tour, for here the self-conscious and elegantly-dressed royal party was surrounded by Indians, many of whom were almost completely naked, coated only in war-paint, and sporting great plumes and feathers. One horseman attracted much attention when he appeared totally covered with yellow paint, save for a few

OPPOSITE: cause for celebration. The people of Ottawa fete the Duke and Duchess of York's visit in September 1901.

daubs of vermilion on his face, and riding a horse streaked with yellow ochre and decorated with feathers. But there was no doubting the sincerity of the welcome. Presenting a copy of the treaty of 1874 whereby the Indians had ceded their independence to Queen Victoria, they expressed their gratitude 'to the Great Spirit for this occasion' and for the opportunity of meeting the 'illustrious grandson of Her Late Majesty Queen Victoria, whose death we most deeply lament'. The Duke presented each Chief with a medal struck on King Edward's orders, to be worn on all ceremonial occasions by them and by their successors.

The tour took the Duke and Duchess from the east to the extreme west of Canada - Vancouver and Victoria were the most westerly stops - and back again via the Niagara Falls. With his now well-known obsession for facts and figures, the Duke dutifully recorded that he shook hands with 24,855 people at official receptions alone, laid 21 foundation stones, received 544 addresses, presented 4,329 medals, gave almost a hundred speeches, and distributed 140 titles. Firework displays heralded the royal couple's arrivals and departures everywhere, and at an evening reception at Saint John, New Brunswick, 'thousands of electric lights turned night into day', according to a local newspaper report. One of the earliest royal walkabouts at Moncton saw the Duke and Duchess stepping from their train and mingling freely with the crowds. The Duke also took time off to shoot game while in the West, and sent back a moose head to HMS *Ophir* to be packed ready for the voyage back to England.

The *Ophir*, after a thorough clean in dry dock, was waiting for the royal party in Halifax, her pristine white hull trimmed with blue, and her buff-coloured, enamel-coated funnels shining in the late autumn sun. Halifax itself was speckled with bunting and flags, and a sizeable crowd saw the Duke and Duchess off, including a large party of Indians - 'most of them in full savage dress', as one crew member observed - who had travelled hundreds of miles to see the royal couple arrive at Halifax and leave again by sea. Snow impeded progress towards Newfoundland, and the *Ophir* had to negotiate icebergs as well as the narrow harbour entrance at St John's during a brief call. Bonfires crackled on high ground, and the message *Welcome to Terra Nova* was painted on the coastal headland. And, never short of imaginative ideas, their hosts sent the royal couple off with a nine-month-old Newfoundland dog harnessed to a mail cart, as a present for their seven-year-old son, Prince Edward. Little did anyone then suspect that this young prince would, in less than two decades' time, take Canada by storm and transform the concept of royal tours almost beyond the recognition of those who so dutifully waved farewell to the Yorks as they set sail for the Mother Country in that autumn of 1901.

OPPOSITE PAGE, TOP LEFT: the Duke and Duchess of Cornwall and York at Government House in September 1901. Governor-General, Lord Minto, and his wife sit either side of the Duchess, whose brother, Prince Alexander of Teck, standing between her and Lord Minto, would himself become Governor-General as Earl of Athlone in 1940. TOP RIGHT: a stately progress through Ottawa. LOWER LEFT: the Duke replies to an address of welcome at Shagannapi Point, Calgary and LOWER RIGHT distributes South African War medals in Calgary's Victoria Park. RIGHT: the royal party take a stroll in Rockcliffe Woods, Ottawa. BELOW: beneath a triumphal arch at Hastings Saw Mill in Vancouver.

ABOVE: the Duke and Duchess of Cornwall and York at Victoria Dock, B.C. at the beginning of October 1901. LEFT: the Duke and Duchess pose for pictures on the Halifax quayside where their ship HMS *Ophir* lies at anchor. BELOW: the royal party at Government House, Toronto; October 11, 1901.

FLEETING BRILLIANCE: THE CONNAUGHTS AND PRINCESS PATRICIA

Less than a decade later, those same royal visitors were King and Queen. Four months after their Coronation, their uncle, the Duke of Connaught, was despatched to Canada for a three-year term as the King's Governor-General, replacing Lord Grey, whose own term of office came to an end in October 1911. The Duke of Connaught, formerly Prince Arthur, the seventh child and third son of Queen Victoria, and later to become the longest lived of all nine of her children, was no stranger to Canada, having paid several visits there since he first crossed the Atlantic in 1869. When, in those early days - just two years after Confederation - he arrived in Nova Scotia, he was a mere nineteen years of age, but his tall, athletic figure, his handsome - if somewhat soulful - features, and his youthful military bearing made him instantly popular. Everywhere he went he was swamped by crowds who confidently evaded police controls and swarmed round his carriage. There was a touch of irony about his brief visit to Fredericton, for which the local organising committee decided to stage a torchlight procession. Unfortunately, they discovered rather late in the day that they lacked a sufficient number of torches and were obliged to go cap-in-hand to the Republican Club at Houlton, just across the border in Maine, to borrow a consignment of torches that had the previous year been used for President Grant's election campaign.

Like his brother before him, Prince Arthur proceeded from the Maritime Provinces to Quebec where he took part in spectacular theatricals and dances at a ball given by the vice-regal couple, and to Montreal where, at a grand pow-wow on an Indian reserve just west of the city, he was made an Iroquois Chief. It was here that he was based with a battalion of the Rifle Brigade, his duties including taking part in an attempt to quell a Fenian raid. But he also spent several months up-country during the autumn and winter, and went on several hunting expeditions in the winter snows. When, eventually, he returned home, he proudly displayed a collection of photographs and woodcuts showing him well togged out in snow shoes and furs, and sleeping in blankets on branches of trees cut down by his Indian hosts.

Needless to say, the very nature of his journey to Canada in 1911, and the fact that he was not only forty-two years older, but also married with three children, made rather different demands on him than his teenage visit in 1869-70, or indeed his other major visit in 1890. The role of Governor-General was always a highly-esteemed one, and Canadians, high on the Coronation festivities of 1911, now enthusiastically welcomed the Duke as the first prince of the blood to preside over their destinies - and little did they know then what their destinies would be in the course of a term of office which would take them into the thick of a world war.

But in that glorious social swansong before the holocaust, there was no end to the celebration of the Duke's arrival, together with his wife, a former Prussian princess, and their younger daughter Princess Patricia. The Duke's elder daughter, Princess Margaret, had married the Crown Prince of Sweden

NATIONAL ARCHIVES OF CANADA/C-14460

Moments of leisure towards the end of a gruelling Empire tour. ABOVE: the Duchess of York, flanked by ladies-in-waiting, takes a walk with the Duke's Private Secretary, Sir Arthur Bigge, at Poplar Point, Manitoba. ABOVE RIGHT: the Duke samples a canoe trip at Senator Kirchoffer's Lake Manitoba shooting lodge. Earlier, the Duchess had experienced the wonder of Banff National Park during a rowing-boat outing across Lake Louise RIGHT.

in 1905, while his son, Prince Arthur, was busy looking for a bride back in England. So the three royal celebrities came to Canada, and travelled first to Quebec. In advance of their arrival, the newspapers were awash with greetings in purple prose and well-meant doggerel, and posters showing the new Governor-General with his wife and daughter, all swathed in the Union Jack, were on sale at every street corner and bookshop. Lending an official gloss to the popular fervour, the Mayor of Quebec suggested that all businesses should close for four hours from midday so that employees and employers alike could take the opportunity to see their new viceroy.

But it didn't all go quite to plan. When the Duke and his family arrived at Quebec station, there was no carriage waiting to take them away, and an embarrassingly long fifteen minutes were endured while the landau was retrieved and brought up into place. When, at last, the royal party were whisked off to their first reception, they were given their first taste of grandiose Canadian hospitality - among two hundred guests described by one journalist as 'the pick of Quebec society of all degrees.'

The royal party then made for Ottawa for the official swearing-in ceremony. Some judicious timing was necessary here, for it was considered desirable for the Governor-General to be out of Quebec by the first instant of the day of the swearing-in, yet logistics decreed that he should not actually arrive in Ottawa until 2.15 pm that day. He and his entourage were therefore taken by train from Quebec just before midnight, and the train was run into a siding just outside the city until the middle of the next morning.

But as at Quebec, the Duke's arrival in Ottawa caught the reception committee napping. This time its was not his carriage, but the guard of honour and accompanying band that failed to turn up at King's Wharf, and the Duke and his family were again kept waiting. Cheerfully, the Duke passed the time by posing for 'a battery of cameras and some moving picture machines' until, eventually, the guard and band arrived and sorted themselves out in a comedy of confusion, panic and apologetic embarrassment. But all that was quickly forgotten as the royal procession made its way to Parliament Hill which was virtually blocked by thousands of men and women running hither and thither across the lawns. At the

Within six months of the Yorks' return to England in 1901, King Edward VII created his son Prince of Wales, and it was as such that he returned to Canada in July 1908 for the Quebec Tercentenary celebrations. TOP: the Prince with members of the crew of his ship HMS *Indomitable*, taking a hand in the boiler room during the voyage to Canada. ABOVE: the Prince and his equerry, Captain Godfrey-Faussett, on their arrival in Quebec. LEFT: the Prince high in the royal box at the tercentenary pageant.

swearing-in ceremony itself, the Duke spoke in French as well as English, though one observer noted that the Dominion Cabinet 'looked bored at having so little to do, and sat very nervously around the red-topped table.'

One of the Duke's earliest duties as Governor-General was to open the twelfth Parliament, an occasion which many likened to a small-scale coronation. Certainly, the socially-conscious invitees may have conceived it as just that - their own national re-run of the grand ceremonies that had taken place back in London a few months before - and the effect was heightened by the sight of the Duchess of Connaught wearing, for the occasion, the very same robe she had worn at King George V's crowning. She carried a dainty little fan instead of a bouquet of flowers, as well as a little case from which, at the appropriate moment, she produced her husband's spectacles for him. But it wasn't quite the placid, measured ceremony that might have been hoped for. Even as it began, the great crush that had, through bad organisation, been caused in the corridors leading to the Parliament chamber had not subsided, and guests trickled in looking rather the worse for wear. Some of the ladies entered looking extremely flustered, with their veils torn to shreds and their bouquets wilting in the overpowering heat. Others came close to fainting and had to be removed into the fresh air to recover. Afterwards, the floors were found to be strewn with shreds of tulle, beads, spangles, crushed flowers and other indications of the fray.

Considering that the Duke's position in the line of royal succession was well into double figures, it seems amazing that there was so much interest in him and his family. On one occasion, the crowds in Toronto were so tightly packed that they spilled out onto the road and into a contingent of Boy Scouts who were about to parade before their Governor-General. The Scouts' flag was accidentally knocked down and trampled underfoot, while the terrified cadets were swallowed up in the crowd and swept off their feet. The same city put on a sparkling ball at the Canadian Yacht Club, which was rated as 'the most brilliant social function in the history of Toronto' - and, having cost $50,000 of pre-World War I money, so it should have been! The Club's colours of blue and gold were festooned everywhere; there were huge areas filled with chrysanthemums, and the hanging lamps were covered in golden gauze.

TOP: ships, royalty and hosts dressed overall as the Prince of Wales disembarks and is welcomed with maximum ceremony to Quebec. ABOVE: the Prince reading his historic and conciliatory tercentenary address to Quebecers at the Champlain Monument. RIGHT: a change of style as the Prince, accompanied by Governor-General Lord Grey and Mgr. Mathieu, Rector of Laval University, motors through Saint-Joachim, near Quebec.

Eventually, the royal party travelled the whole breadth of Canada, reaching Victoria by 1912, and making as early an acquaintance with all their subjects as they could. Like others before and after them, they made full use of the leisure facilities offered by their surroundings. The Duke and Duchess learned to ski on the hills at Rockliffe; the Duchess in particular loved ice-skating, at which she excelled, and she followed in her husband's footsteps by perfecting her shooting skills. During a visit to Alberta, in fact, she had to apply for a licence, under the Game Act of 1907, to 'hunt, take and kill game birds'. And she had to pay her $5 fee!

In October 1913, the family returned briefly to Britain to attend the wedding of the Connaught's son Prince Arthur, to his cousin, Princess Alexandra of Fife, King Edward VII's eldest grandchild. The following year, with the advent of war, and just short of the the end of the Duke's three-year appointment, it was expected that the Duke would have to return to Europe again - and for good - to take up command of his regiment. The King had already decided that his own brother-in-law, Prince Alexander of Teck, should succeed the Duke as Governor-General, and both the Duke and the now ageing Princess Louise had briefed Prince Alexander about their prospective new duties. But both the King and the

Duke reckoned without the sense of commitment that Prince Alexander felt towards his own military career, which led to his polite but firm insistence to the King that his first duty in the anticipation of war was to the 2nd Life Guards, of which he was second-in-command. The King at first refused to agree, and was finally convinced only by Prince Alexander's explanation that the Duke of Connaught was really too old for active service, and would be of far greater use to Canada, with whose land and people he was by now thoroughly familiar. As we shall see, Prince Alexander's turn would come: as Earl of Athlone, he was to serve as Canada's Governor-General for the duration of the Second World War.

The King's decision to keep the Duke of Connaught at his post was well-received by the Canadians, but while he remained popular throughout the remainder of his term, his increasing

BELOW LEFT: the Duke and Duchess of Connaught greeted on arriving in Canada in 1911. BELOW: the Duke and Duchess, with Princess Patricia, visit Montreal General Hospital in 1911. BOTTOM: the Connaughts and their staff at Ottawa in 1912.

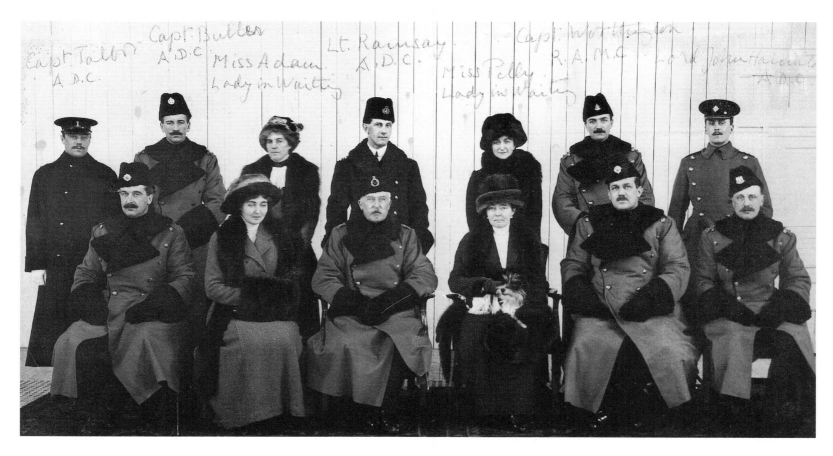

insistence on being consulted, or having his advice followed, on questions relating to the management of wartime military matters, earned him few friends in the Canadian government. Prime Minister Borden found him exasperatingly opinionated and accusations flew that the Duke was stretching his constitutional powers to the utmost. Nevertheless, when, in 1915, it was mooted that the Duke should go back to England to command the British Home Defence Army, the *Montreal Gazette* printed an editorial in which it sincerely hoped it wouldn't happen, and that 'his term, already extended beyond the time set when the appointment was announced, will be continued until the war is over, and he can be welcomed home after a well-won victory of the army he has helped to create and inspire.'

The Duchess of Connaught enjoyed indifferent health during the latter years of the family's stay in Canada, a circumstance which was not helped by the opprobrium with which all Prussians were viewed, and which made it fortunate

LEFT: the Duke and Duchess on board a yacht, 1912. BELOW: the Duke of Connaught is installed as Governor-General, October 13, 1911.

that much of the Connaughts' popularity was, it has to be said, due to the presence of their twenty-five-year-old daughter, Princess Patricia. She had the advantage of youth as well as a demure beauty, and her arrival in Canada prompted one newspaper to greet her with the averral that she was 'the only princess in Great Britain who is really pretty, clever and witty, as well as young.' She charmed the Canadians, just as Princess Diana would do three-quarters of a century later, and the little gestures counted most. At Toronto's Hospital for Sick Children, for instance, she pulled little sprigs of ferns and flower from her bouquet and distributed them to some of the young patients, and in Quebec she pulled a Christmas cracker with every child at a party she attended. At another Christmas party she was, far from being offended, highly amused to hear that the local Temperance Society had insisted that the Christmas pudding should be withdrawn from the menu because it was laced with alcohol!

She was a proficient skier, and the outdoor-loving Canadians were impressed by the degree to which a few seasons in Alpine Europe had perfected her skills. She was an accomplished painter, as Princess Louise had been before her, and she made several forays to different parts of Canada to capture the country's breathtaking scenery in paints and oils. Three such pictures she exhibited at the 1912, and two more at the 1914, exhibitions of the Royal Canadian Academy, which her father opened. She stocked the walls of her sitting room with her sketches, and when she eventually returned to England, she exhibited some of her oil paintings of Canadian life in London.

Canada's most significant gesture to Princess Patricia was to name a newly formed regiment after her - Princess Patricia's Canadian Light Infantry - and she returned the compliment by designing the regimental badge and Colour, which she also helped to work. By this time she was receiving compliments of every kind, such as the following anonymous Christmas greeting in a verse of all too evidently home-made poetry, too dreadful ever to be consigned to the legion of the lost:

Pulchritudinous Princess Patricia,
A right merry Christmas we wish yer,
Your champions at call
Are Canadians all,
Civilians as well as militia.

For her, the five years in Canada were blissfully happy. In her father's entourage was a thirty-year-old naval lieutenant, the Honourable Alexander Ramsay. He and the Princess began a long and close friendship that outlasted both the Duke's Governor-Generalship and the war. In 1919, they were married, and Princess Patricia, who had given her royal name to so many Canadian schools, institutions and regiments, gave it up to marry the man she loved. She became simply Lady Patricia Ramsay; she lived to be the last survivor but one of all Queen Victoria's forty grandchildren; and she and her husband lived together quietly, happily and long enough to celebrate their golden wedding anniversary. One wonders how often they reflected on those early years in Canada, where their long-lasting affection for each other took root.

'PUT IT THERE, ED!': THE AMBASSADOR PRINCE

In his farewell letter to the Governor-General at the end of his 1901 tour, the future King George V had written of his 'imperishable memories of affectionate loyal hearts, frank and independent natures, prosperous and progressive communities, boundless productive territories, glorious scenery, stupendous works of nature, and a people and country proud of their membership of the Empire, and in which the Empire finds one of its brightest offspring'. After the cessation of European hostilities in 1918, the King's own offspring paid several visits to Canada in their turn, and the first and most famous of these visits was that of his eldest, Edward, Prince of Wales, in 1919. Conceived as the first of several grand Empire tours, it was one of four he made to Canada, two of which, though each lasting well over a month, were unofficial.

The Prince was twenty-five years of age when he first set foot in the Dominion, and his less than biddable behaviour *vis-à-vis* his parents prompted the King, like Prince Albert before him, to add an older, patriarchal Establishment figure (this time in the shape of Rear-Admiral Sir Lionel Halsey) to his son's retinue. It was illustrative of the relationship between father and son that the Prince was less inclined to the King's stolid, Victorian concept of the tour than to Lloyd George's vision of it as 'if not a vaudeville show, a first-class carnival' in which the Prince should display 'a many-sided and natural role'.

The former idea certainly materialised in the endless programme of State drives, mounted parades, civic lunches, after-dinner speeches and the laying of foundation stones - the most important of which was in connection with the Victoria Tower, now called the Peace Tower, in Ottawa. All of which soon made it clear to the Prince that unless he changed matters, the tour would be run very much in line with his father's 1901 visit. But in the event, any pretensions

to pomposity were soon exposed when, on his arrival at St John's, Newfoundland, he noticed that the triumphal arch under which he walked in procession was built of drums containing cod-liver oil and festooned with dried fish carcases!

This somewhat irreverent observation (which matched his earlier, and equally irreverent behaviour in taking a little shooting practice against passing icebergs on his ship's entry into Canadian waters) and the amazing but enjoyable discovery of the effusive vigour of volatile crowds in Quebec made him realise that a novel and more original royal response was required. Amused, if faintly alarmed, by the way the Quebecois repeatedly broke through police cordons to snatch at his tie or handkerchief, or to tear his buttons from his new coat, he was quick to brush aside his organisers' helpless and abject apology - 'I simply cannot understand what has come over the Canadian people, Sir' - and he made a straightforward but ardent plea for a revision of the arrangements in favour of a less formal programme.

The request was resisted until, at the Toronto Exhibition Grounds, a Warriors Day horseback review of those who had just come back from the War turned into a scrummage as the cheering veterans suddenly broke ranks, surged round the Prince, lifted him from his horse, and passed him, 'like a football', over their heads till he eventually reached the dais. Thenceforth, formality was kept to a minimum. It was in Toronto, too, that a chance remark by one war veteran during a presentation - 'Put it there, Ed: I shook hands with your grand-dad' - led the Prince to make himself available at all future events to meet anybody who cared to come up and shake hands with him. But that plan backfired. Time constraints made it necessary to call a halt on successive occasions, and in any case it took only a week for the Prince's right hand to become so black, swollen and painful from the

LEFT: the Duchess displays her skating skills. ABOVE: the Connaughts on tour: the Duke and Duchess on their CPR train, with their staff and (2nd from right) Mr

Baker of the CPR. BELOW: Duke, Duchess and Princess Patricia (with muff) in the Canadian countryside, winter 1912-13.

RIGHT: Edward, Prince of Wales being driven through an arch of welcome made of dried fish carcases and oil barrels at St John's, Newfoundland in August 1919. BELOW: at Quebec, the Prince pins the DCM on a French Canadian whose son won it in the Great War but never lived to wear it. BELOW RIGHT: the most famous picture: the Prince of Wales, cigarette between lips, grins as he signs a visiting book in Nova Scotia.

NATIONAL ARCHIVES OF CANADA/PA–22261

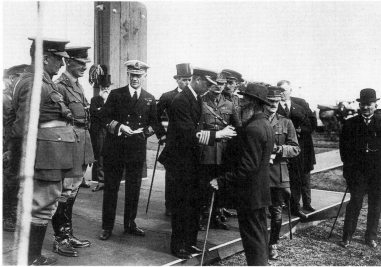

NATIONAL ARCHIVES OF CANADA/C–3213

NATIONAL ARCHIVES OF CANADA/PA–22340

NATIONAL ARCHIVES OF CANADA/C–3211

LEFT: the Prince inspecting veterans in Halifax in August 1919. OPPOSITE PAGE BOTTOM: a scene typical of most during the Prince of Wales' first tour. Dense crowds, such as these in Ottawa, a motorcade hardly able to progress through them, and a young royal celebrity waving his hat in response to deafening cheers – all were daily ingredients of a tour which impressed both the Prince and those who saw him.

continued enthusiastic handshaking that, in his own words, he 'retired it temporarily from Imperial service, and offered the left instead'.

Thirty years later, as Duke of Windsor, he was to describe that tour as 'the most exhilarating I have ever known', and its tone led him to make significant modifications to the accepted habit of royal speechmaking, as well as physical contact with the public. At first, he found little difficulty in making the right noises. The themes of national and Empire unity, though conceivably a stuffy one from the point of view of this 25-year-old, was well worked during the tour. At Montreal, for instance, the Prince pressed the issue in an address to an audience which combined French and English Canadians. 'The union of the two races in Canada was never a matter of mere political convenience,' he said. 'The union of England and Scotland has been in existence for nearly two centuries. Who can doubt that the union of Canada will produce as great, as powerful and as united a nation as the British nation itself?'

On other occasions, extending the theme to embrace the role of the Royal Family at the head of a unity of Dominions, he adapted it to apply to his own personal position. 'The Dominions are no longer colonies,' he said at Toronto, for example. 'They are sister nations of the British nation, and their international importance will steadily increase. That is the reason why I do not regard myself as belonging primarily to Great Britain and only in a lesser way to Canada. On the contrary, I regard myself as belonging to Great Britain and to Canada in exactly the same way. This means that when I go down to the United States next week, I shall regard myself as going there not only as an Englishman and as a Britisher, but also as a Canadian and as a representative of the whole Empire.'

That approach had of course been drilled into him by his mentors, but he himself began to change the emphasis when circumstances allowed. The train which took him ten thousand miles to over fifty towns in three months was fitted with an observation platform so that communities from settlements all along the track could clearly see him. Often their

TOP: the Prince *al fresco*: on the banks of the Nipigon River with a local guide, and ready for the shoot. LEFT: smile please! The Prince pauses for an amateur photographer during a reception at Winnipeg in September 1919.

NATIONAL ARCHIVES OF CANADA/C-3217

enthusiasm persuaded drivers to halt the train, and the Prince was called upon to speak to loyal groups of spectators. In time, he evolved a convenient, standard three-minute speech, interlaced with useful local facts which had been supplied to him only minutes before by his staff. But he soon found that, as he himself put it, 'on more than one occasion, disconcerting bursts of laughter instead of the customary applause informed me that I had made the lamentable blunder of confusing my audience with a rival community some distance down the track.' So, as an antidote to these risks, he took to the idea of using these enforced halts to get off the train, stretch his legs and chat informally with the locals, be they miners, farmers, industrial workers, or whoever. This pleasing and popular approach taught him more about those he had come to visit than anything he could learn from notes given to him by his entourage, or from set speeches loyally delivered to him in more formal surroundings.

Needless to say, the Canadians responded magnificently to his personal touch, and no-one seemed to enjoy it all more than he. Legends in words and pictures were created during those three months: the report of the war veteran who fought with police to establish his right to meet the Prince personally; the story of how, when the cap of a wounded chair-bound soldier was whisked off by the wind, the Prince sprinted after it, retrieved it, and placed it back on its owner's head; the enduring photograph of the sailor Prince signing an official Visitors' Book, with a cigarette cocked jauntily between his lips; another picture of him resplendent in the full feathered headdress of an Indian Chief after he had been proclaimed Chief Morning Star by the Stony Indians of Alberta; the experience of seeing him graduate from spectator to performer at an exhibition of bronco-busting at Saskatoon, where he acquitted himself by staying the full course. He drove his own locomotive - CPR 2231 - from Flavelle to Thorold in Ontario, joined a cattle round-up and cut out a herd at the Bar U Ranch in Alberta, went duck-shooting at Qu'Appelle Lake in Saskatchewan, and spent a few days at an Indian camp near the Nipigon river, eating Indian food, canoeing, and fishing for trout.

It was only a matter of time, therefore, before he would declare that, for a real holiday, Canada would be his first choice, and the thought impelled him to buy 1,600, and lease a further 2,400, acres of land at Pekisko High River, seventy

ABOVE: three cheers for the King! The Prince of Wales responding to loyal hosts in High Park, Toronto.
OPPOSITE PAGE, TOP: helping with the round-up at Bar-U Ranch near High River, Alberta. At Banff, the

Prince was made an Indian Chief and OPPOSITE PAGE, BOTTOM replies to an initiation address from the Stony Indians.

miles south of Calgary, which, named after his own formal initials, he called the EP Ranch. Leisure-wise, the ranch was extremely important to him: he found it a haven 'where I would find occasional escape from the sometimes too confining, too well-ordered island life in Britain.' At the same time, it was here that, wishing to 'make available the best of English and Scottish blood in Shorthorn cattle, Clydesdale horses and Hampshire sheep to the farming of Canada', he imported and reared these animals to create a successful concern by 1927.

By 1930 he had invested a total of $250,000 in the property and its operations, but the disastrous effects of the economic blight of the ensuing decade upon farming convinced him that he should sell. The Canadian government viewed with some horror that prospect, which carried with it the potential loss of excellent stock as well as of prestige, and only by offering the Prince several thousand additional acres of neighbouring Crown land in 1932 did they persuade him to stay. Even so, he continued to make losses year by year, right up to to outbreak of war.

He had applied for a licence to work minerals in 1930, and the discovery of oil in a nearby valley ten years later convinced him that better times were on the way. The 1932 grant of land fortunately carried with it the right to take oil, and having turned down an offer of $40,000 for the original property in 1940 the Duke began to pump tens of thousands of precious dollars into the exploitation programme. By 1945, he was advised that drilling should begin, and when the first oil eventually spouted, he was delighted. But it was a short-lived joy: the oil turned to water, and the work and hopes of fifteen years came to a very expensive nothing. Philosophical though he was at this bitter disappointment, he rarely visited the ranch after that. His short fishing holiday in Canada at the end of the war was confined to New Brunswick, and although

he paid a nostalgic call to the property in 1951, he was in little mood to push the enterprise on. He sold it for a reported $190,000 in 1962 - a mere fraction of its overall cost to him since its purchase, and poor compensation for the years of running losses that the 1929 Crash and the oil failure had brought in their wake.

Four years after his first, and memorably successful visit to Canada, the Prince of Wales was back again, but this time in a purely private capacity. In the late autumn of 1923, he travelled from Quebec to his ranch, calling in at most of the provincial capitals *en route*, and spending several days in Banff, Montreal and Ottawa on the way back. A year later, he paid another autumn visit to the ranch, again making this part of a grand social tour, with just the occasional morning, afternoon or evening being given over to more formal duties. By that time, he had discovered a new love - that of hunting - and had acquired quite a reputation as a keen and sportsmanlike rider. One of his party, Charles Morris, could not praise him enough: 'He rides loose and well,' wrote Morris, 'and we could not lose him anywhere we went. He was always on my skirts, and I do think if he'd had better luck, he could have overridden me many times, but he was too good a sportsman to do that.' The occasion was a ride with the Toronto and Eglington Hunt, during which, when taking a fence, the Prince had one of many tumbles that had the Establishment back in Britain fearing for his life.

His second official visit in 1927, made in the company of his youngest surviving brother, Prince George, and of British Prime Minister Stanley Baldwin, was a more formal business than the first. Involving his attendance at the celebrations marking the Diamond Jubilee of the Confederation, and a visit to almost forty towns and cities, it also incorporated the inauguration of the Peace Bridge across the Niagara Falls in a ceremony which had the Prince and the Vice-President of America walking across the bridge from opposite ends, meeting in the middle, and then cutting a silk cord. The tour itself had a disconcerting start. The Governor-General, for whom horse-

driving was an absorbing pastime, had decided to take the two Princes to the official residence by open landau pulled by two horses. The Prince of Wales, who had, on his previous official visit, made known his dislike of this form of transport, was furious, but not nearly so much as when the horses bolted during the journey. Not without difficulty were they brought under control, and the ride ended without further incident or personal injury. But the Governor-General was unapologetic, inviting the Princes' congratulations on the quality of his liveliest pair of horses!

After the official part of the tour, the Prince of Wales and his brother journeyed with Mr Baldwin as far west as Calgary, and the friendship they struck up was to have significant implications nine years later, at the height of the Abdication crisis. As indeed would the memory in the Canadian mind of all those delightfully informal visits he made before he became King, and which remained ineradicable for years afterwards. 'He really is idolized here', wrote the Governor-General, Lord Tweedsmuir, almost justifying the vacillating attitude of the Canadian authorities at the time of the Abdication. 'Canada feels that he is her own possession'. Those may have been the sentiments of the British patriot who also happened to be Canada's Governor-General, but the feeling among Canadians generally was that the Prince had made Canada his second home and Canadians his compatriots. And of course, they were proud of the honour.

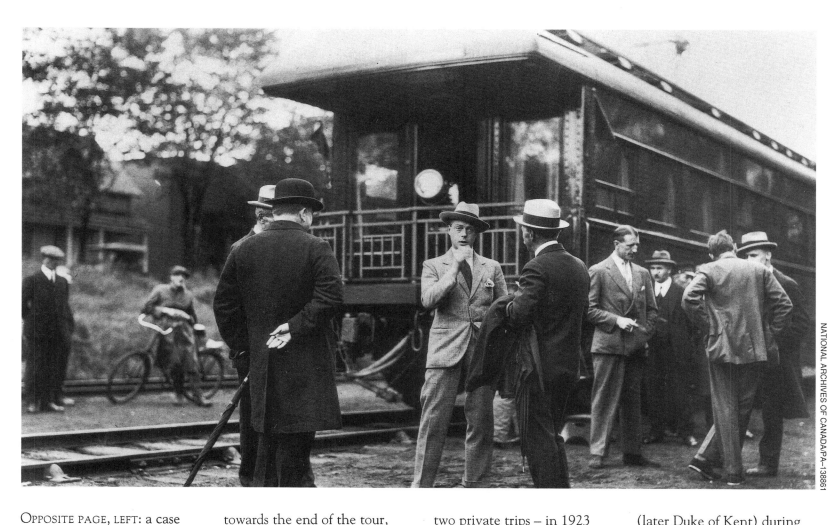

NATIONAL ARCHIVES OF CANADA/PA–138861

OPPOSITE PAGE, LEFT: a case of over-enthusiasm: officials turn away an autograph-hunter during the 1919 tour; TOP RIGHT: the Prince shook so many hands during his tour that his right hand became bruised and painful. In thanking the royal train staff for their services towards the end of the tour, he uses his left hand instead; LOWER RIGHT: the Prince of Wales duck-hunting in Qu'Appele Valley, Saskatchewan, October 1919. THIS PAGE, ABOVE: between his official visits to Canada in 1919 and 1927, the Prince of Wales made two private trips – in 1923 and 1924. Here, he stretches his legs along the Canadian National Railway lines at Ottawa during his 1924 visit and BELOW LEFT chats with Prime Minister Mackenzie King. BELOW: the Prince of Wales with his favourite brother, Prince George (later Duke of Kent) during their tour of 1927.

NATIONAL ARCHIVES OF CANADA/C–14184

ABOVE: the Prince of Wales (right, with Mackenzie King) at the unveiling of the statue of Sir Wilfrid Laurier in Ottawa, 1927. LEFT: opening the Peace Bridge across the Niagara River. BELOW: the Prince takes a break at Laval-sur-le-Lac Golf Club, Montreal.

GEORGE AND ELIZABETH: THE BEGINNING OF A BEAUTIFUL FRIENDSHIP

The confusing and often bitter memories of the Abdication and its aftermath were well and truly forgotten by the time of the next major royal visit to Canada. Just over two years after their accession, the new King George VI and his popular consort Queen Elizabeth, now the Queen Mother, embarked on an exhausting and comprehensive seven-week tour which in many respects followed the sequence and general route of their predecessors. They travelled from coast to coast in memorably superb weather, and the colour, dazzle and intensity of their reception at every level quickly eclipsed their much-publicised, brilliant though brief State Visit to France the previous year.

The issues of peace and war prevailing at the time brought two major influences to bear on the tour. First, it was covertly conceived as a means of persuading Canadians into the way of committing themselves in advance to a war which, despite the often controversial efforts then being exerted by the British government to prevent it, many in power throughout the world knew would soon begin. Secondly, and almost perversely, the tour was very nearly called off because of the heightened tension of the European political situation at the time of the Czechoslovakian crisis. Lord Tweedsmuir was vociferous in urging that the tour should on no account be cancelled and, in events, there was no delay to the King and Queen's departure from England, although the lately-perceived need to retain as many warships in Britain against a prospective outbreak of hostilities meant that HMS *Repulse*, the proposed royal transport ship, had to stay in home waters, while the liner *Empress of Australia* was swiftly substituted .

As luck would have it, the liner almost came to grief during its leisurely voyage across the Atlantic, during which both the King and Queen shot a vast amount of film with their newly-acquired movie cameras. 'We very nearly hit an iceberg the day before yesterday,' the Queen wrote to her 71-year-old mother-in-law Queen Mary, 'and the poor Captain was nearly demented because some kind, cheerful people kept reminding him that it was about here that the *Titanic* was struck - and just about the same date.' The captain's sense of panic was presumably not greatly relieved by the news that, during the lull that followed, the Chief Purser's canary laid its very first egg! In fact, drifting ice-floes and murky weather held them up for some time, but on 17th May 1939, they berthed safely but belatedly at Quebec.

In a sense, Canada was not new to the King. Not only had he learned a great deal of his parents' and brothers' experiences in this forward-looking and vibrant Dominion, but he had also visited the country himself - way back in 1913 - during a six-month training voyage aboard the cruiser *Cumberland*, which also took him to Tenerife and the Caribbean. When his ship arrived in Canada in those last months of peacetime, for a series of courtesy calls to several Canadian and Newfoundland ports, he alone of the ship's company was swamped by wildly cheering crowds and pestered by newspaper reporters each seeking their first royal interview scoop story. As one might expect in those days of stiffish royal protocol, the young and fairly untried naval trainee did not play ball. Instead, he and his shipmates made Canada their oyster, visiting the Toronto sights, shooting the rapids between Niagara and Montreal, and being shown around Ontario power station - 'the voltage is 60,000 volts and they can generate with thirteen water turbines,' he wrote, rather ploddingly, to his parents back home. He went salmon fishing in Newfoundland, and attended dances which various organisations arranged for the visiting crew, at one of which,

BELOW: George VI lands at Quebec on May 17, 1939 for the first Canadian tour by a reigning monarch.

NATIONAL ARCHIVES OF CANADA/C-6637

in Montreal, his Commander tactfully spent all his time ensuring that the Prince was provided with an equal number of English- and French-speaking Canadian partners! The essential informality of this visit gave the reserved, self-conscious 17-year old Prince Albert (as he was then known) his first real boost of self-confidence, and the breadth and excitement of his experience afforded Canada a special place in his affections ever since.

When, on that May day of 1939, the slight, modest and unassuming figure of King George, now in his 44th year, landed at Quebec, he achieved the distinction of becoming the first reigning sovereign to set foot upon Canadian soil. It was a distinction as arbitrary as any, but it meant everything to loyal, welcoming Canadians whose sometimes quite frenetic participation made the tour the resounding success it was, and certainly gave it a character that amazed and absorbed the royal visitors' British subjects back in Britain for many weeks. Without doubt, the decision to develop what was originally intended as a short trip to Ottawa into a full-blown royal tour was a happy one, and many still alive in Canada who hold precious memories of their special moment in it.

On a wider level, perhaps the most enduring memory, and indeed symbol, of the tour was the 300-ton blue and aluminium CPR locomotive that steamed across the country with its royal passengers and their entourage, luggage and accumulating gifts, all just about contained in a total of a dozen streamlined coaches. The 'silver and blue train', as it became familiarly known, completed its stop-go journey of over 9,000 miles from Quebec to Vancouver, and back to Halifax in forty days. At every station - and with a full programme which left very little time for relaxation, their number seemed countless - there was a crowd to greet the King and Queen. The visitors responded in kind. They had given instructions that they were to be alerted whenever well-wishers were spotted by the side of the railway track, so that their long wait could be rewarded. Indeed this novel aspect of the royal visit posed fashion problems for Queen Elizabeth, who soon became

On May 19, two days after they had arrived in Canada, King George VI and Queen Elizabeth were entertained at one of the most sumptuous banquets of their entire tour. Given by the City of Montreal, it set a standard of magnificence that was hard to equal. ABOVE: part of the colossal banqueting hall, the King and Queen in the centre background. BELOW: still in evening dress, the royal visitors leave Montreal's Windsor Street Station for Ottawa.

accustomed to being awakened at night or earliest dawn to appear on the train's observation platform and acknowledge impromptu local demonstrations of loyalty. What to wear, on those sudden and unscheduled stops, to combine convenience, dignity and flair? The House of Hartnell came up with the perfect solution - a long, flowing negligee trimmed lightly with sable, that could easily be thrown over night-clothes with speed, ease and decorum!

Like most, this tour had its formal and informal moments. Of the former, the laying of the foundation stone of the new Supreme Court building in Ottawa was for the Queen perhaps the most memorable. With her slightly mischievous sense of humour, she mused on the fact that she, and not the King, had been asked to perform the ceremony, deeming this, with her special knack of coming to an irrefutable conclusion, to be an appropriate decision, since, as she put it, 'woman's position in modern society has depended upon the growth of law.' How things have changed since! Among the more informal interludes of the tour were her extempore ten-minute chat, right in the middle of another stone-laying ceremony, with a group of Scottish stonemasons, while officials and crowds wondered what had caused the hold-up; and the King and Queen's private visit to see the famous Dionne quins who had, in what many still regard (for those days of rare multiple births) as virtually miraculous circumstances, been born five years earlier.

The Queen herself was credited with her own brand of miracle-making when, despite a rare bout of persistent rain

TOP: the King, in Field-Marshal's uniform, and Queen on the Parliament steps in Ottawa at the opening of Parliament, and LEFT enthroned in the Senate Chamber flanked by members of both Houses during the ceremony. Later, in front of the Parliament Buildings BELOW, the King took the Salute at Trooping the Colour. BELOW LEFT: the royal motorcade arriving at the site of the new Supreme Court building in Ottawa's Wellington Street.

NATIONAL ARCHIVES OF CANADA/C-30805

NATIONAL ARCHIVES OF CANADA/C-53469

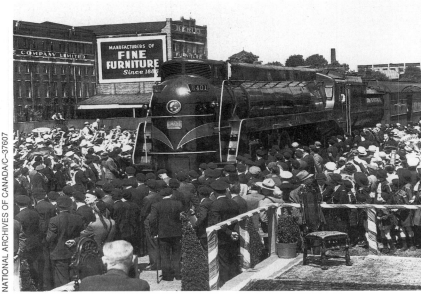

ABOVE LEFT: 'The first British King and Queen to go really democratic and mingle with the hoi polloi.' So one journalist described the royal guests as they walked into the crowds in Ottawa to speak with veterans. ABOVE: the royal train that took the royal party from coast to coast, here seen at Kitchener, Ontario. LEFT: the King reviews the Vancouver Highlanders in British Columbia. ABOVE RIGHT: arriving at the grandstand of Woodbine Racetrack – the first of many such visits for the Queen. RIGHT: the King and Queen riding in a democrat through Banff National Park, Alberta. OPPOSITE PAGE: enjoying a break at Outlook Cottage, Jasper Park Lodge, Alberta.

during a drive through Winnipeg, she instructed that the car roof should be let down so that people could see her more easily. Almost immediately, the rain stopped! It all seemed to add the personal magic that she wove during that momentous tour. 'A Queen who smiles like an angel,' was how one commentator put it, while another enthused: 'As for the Queen, she appeared - and the day was won. So simple in her bearing, and yet so refined, so spontaneous in every move and yet so harmonious, so radiant with feminine charm and so expressive of emotion, she also found the true words for every occasion and every person.' It sounds pretty gushing by today's standards, but the royal admirer whose words have worn well down the generations has yet to be born.

Lord Tweedsmuir, still Canada's Governor-General, praised the royal couple's creditable acquittal of their duties in more perceptive terms, and with the grateful sincerity of one to whom the organisation of such a massive enterprise proved well worth the effort. He singled the Queen out for special praise, as one who had 'a perfect genius for the right kind of publicity. The unrehearsed episodes were marvellous,' he

continued, describing how popular she had been for ignoring the set programme so frequently and unexpectedly, and wandering towards the crowds to meet them personally. The royal visitors enjoyed the tour, too. 'It made us,' the Queen confided to Prime Minister Mackenzie King, mindful of the uncertain and delicate circumstances in which her husband had come to the Throne, and she was no doubt highly delighted that her impeccable French, well learned in childhood, had, as in Paris the previous year, put her on an excellent footing with French-speaking communities throughout the country. As for the King, he presumably thought his tour very much worth while when he heard one provincial premier's assurance that 'you can go home and tell the old country that any talk they may hear about Canada being isolationist is just nonsense.' That certainly proved to be the case, and it may have been more than just convenience that led the King, the following year, to opt for another royal Governor-General to consolidate the loyalty and personal affection that Canada and Canadians undoubtedly felt toward their counterparts across the Atlantic.

During the Earl of Athlone's Governor-Generalship, the Duke of Kent carried out, in 1941, a tour of service bases, as in Vancouver, where TOP LEFT he visited shipyards and met repair hands. ABOVE: Princess Alice meets Indian representatives in Vancouver, 1941. LEFT: the Athlones in the grounds of their home in England shortly after the Earl's appointment in April 1940. BELOW LEFT: with family and staff at Rideau Hall during the Duke of Kent's visit in August 1941. BELOW: Lord Athlone inspecting the 140th 25-pounder gun cast at Sorel, P.Q. in December 1941. OPPOSITE PAGE: the Duke of Kent meets Chief Johnny Bearspaw (left) while visiting Banff in August 1941.

THE ATHLONE YEARS: A WARTIME GOVERNOR-GENERAL

In 1940, the year after King George VI and Queen Elizabeth's tour, Lord Tweedsmuir died, and Mackenzie King asked whether he might submit to the King the name of the Earl of Athlone as Canada's next Governor-General. Lord Athlone was the King's uncle, the youngest, and by then the sole survivor, of Queen Mary's three brothers. George VI was quietly pleased with this suggestion with its flattering implications of loyalty towards the Royal Family. Lord Athlone, on the contrary, was in two minds. On the one hand, the appointment would consummate the efforts made by others for him to fill the post back in 1914, and would certainly compensate for the postponement of a proposed visit to Canada early in 1936 when King George V's final illness made it imperative for the Athlones to be at Queen Mary's side at Sandringham. On the other hand, the Earl was by now 65 and a five-year term would take him into his seventies. Eventually he compromised his reservations by accepting the post for two years only, hoping 'in spite of all, that I shall be able to carry out the work'.

Initially 'the work' proved to be the least of his problems. There was, to begin with, the little matter of actually getting to Canada in wartime conditions, across a hostile Atlantic Ocean, peppered with German U-boats. Sure enough, the voyage turned into an overlong and circuitous dodge between real, suspected or anticipated German ships and submarines. Nevertheless, with him went his jolly wife, Princess Alice; she, the only daughter of Queen Victoria's youngest son Prince Leopold, was destined to become the old Queen's last surviving grand-daughter and - dying in 1981, only seven weeks before her 98th birthday - the oldest ever member of the British Royal Family.

Princess Alice proved her unusual perceptive self right from the moment she arrived in June 1940 in Ottawa - via Halifax which had, predictably for a royal visit, been awash with heavy rain. 'Many people were there to look at us', she recorded, 'but as always they were undemonstrative'. But, notwithstanding the reticence of the crowds, the assaults of the weather, and the shortage of staff owing to the conscription of young men for the war effort, the Athlones set about the business of settling in with speed and vigour. Rearranging furniture became a frequent pastime; changing colour schemes became almost a challenge in the absence of materials due to wartime European shortages, and Princess Alice was reduced to dyeing scores of old mauve satin curtains and drapes - which the Tweedsmuirs, whose favourite colour it was, had left in almost every room - because she simply couldn't stand the old colour any longer! Always an expert gardener, as her namesake Princess Alice of Gloucester will readily testify, she overcame the restriction of the short Ottawa summers by designing and helping to build rock gardens, and by keeping five hot-houses running in order to produce beautiful plants and flowers even in the extremes of winter climate.

Lord Athlone meanwhile took up his job with an unsurpassed and unquestioning sense of duty. His earnest application brought him into frequent conflict with Mackenzie King, the risk of which was accentuated by the Prime Minister's equally frequent conflicts with his own Cabinet - conflicts which, in their turn, led Athlone to attempt to reconcile the parties for the sake of unity and efficiency. Though Mackenzie King appreciated his Governor-General's charm, discretion and lack of affectation, he came in time to regret his recommendation in favour of Lord Athlone when it became apparent that the latter was not prepared merely to pass on the nod everything the former did or suggested. Indeed, the Prime Minister eventually began to resent having someone "not

belonging to one's own country" intruding upon his domain, however unaffectedly. In addition, neither man was renowned for his docile temper, and Princess Alice always feared the worst when she heard their raised voices at Rideau Hall.

Meanwhile, conscious of the need to see and be seen, the Athlones made several trips to all parts of the country throughout their term of office, which in spite of the Earl's initial expectations, lasted throughout the war. In that time they saw the glorious valley scenery around Jasper, inspected the glacier 2,000 feet up on Mount Edith Cavell, stayed on Vancouver Island, quartered in a log hut with stupendous sea and forest views, were overawed by the later summer beauty of New Brunswick and saw flocks of snow geese at Cape Tourmente. They visited Lake Louise - a poignant pilgrimage, since the first royal Governor-General's wife had died only shortly before the war at the ripe old age of 91 - and found this 'jewel of the Rockies' delightful, though 'spoilt by the hideous hotel' recently built there. During a visit to Fort William on Lake Superior, Lord Athlone was dubbed Chief Rainbow of the Ojibway tribe, and was obliged to dance around a ceremonial fire in full tribal trappings. Princess Alice joined in the fun and put on a squaw's headdress - a task she found not wholly to her liking as 'I hate having to remove my hat without a mirror'! They crossed the border to visit President Roosevelt at Hyde Park on the Hudson River, and in turn hosted Roosevelt and Churchill at their official Quebec residence, The Citadel, for each of the two important wartime Quebec conferences.

Lord Athlone's Governor-Generalship turned out to be comparatively uneventful and largely smooth-going. His only fear for Canadian unity and the national war effort arose out of the potential sympathy felt by the French-speaking Quebecois for the Vichy government which, of course, was tantamount to being an enemy of Britain. Fortunately, the Roman Catholic Church in Quebec was strongly anti-Nazi,

and succeeded in keeping the province calm and at least superficially pro-British.

That apart, the main influence of the European - and eventually world - war upon the Athlones was of a more domestic nature. Their first consignment of Christmas cards, for instance, disappeared without trace while being shipped to Britain. Some of their more remote family ties were strengthened as streams of European royalty headed for the Dominion after the German invasions of mid-1940. The Dutch Crown Princess Juliana came with her husband, Prince Bernhardt, and their children, Beatrix and Irene, to stay at Government House as the Athlones' guests, having come from Holland via Buckingham Palace where baby Irene had just been christened. Shortly afterwards, the Athlones welcomed Juliana's mother, Queen Wilhelmina, a first cousin, on the maternal side, to Princess Alice herself. Later, they received the ex-Empress Zita of Austria, still wearing the same black, swathed dress she had worn since being widowed almost twenty years before, along with members of her numerous family, all of whom stayed for some time at Government House.

Another royal visitor was Prince George, Duke of Kent, who in 1941 arrived in a Liberator to begin a tour of thousands of miles, inspecting Commonwealth Air Training centres,

and visiting RAF Ferry command in Montreal. In doing so, he became the first member of the Royal Family to fly the Atlantic. Ironically, he was killed while flying from England to Iceland almost exactly a year later.

His elder brother, the Duke of Windsor, also called in on his aunt and uncle on his way to the EP Ranch, though not without a great deal of frustrated effort on his part. Ever since his Abdication, the Duke had wanted to visit his ranch, but the Canadian government, possibly prompted by the British authorities and by knowledge of the Royal Family's attitude towards the Windsors, refused to allow him in. When, in 1940, the Duke became Governor of the Bahamas, he immediately applied to the wartime British government for permission to visit Canada, in order to get away from the intensely humid climate of the Bahamas in summer, and to allow time for his official residence in Nassau to be renovated. Though permission was refused, it was granted on a second application a year later when the Duke, desperate to see the ranch - 'the only home I ever owned' - again, after over a decade, managed to convince Churchill of the innocence of his intentions. Initially, it was not envisaged that the Duke and Duchess would be visiting the Athlones at Government House: 'Needless to say,' wrote the Duchess to her aunt with just a hint of venom, 'we do not go anywhere near Government

OPPOSITE PAGE, UPPER LEFT: the Athlones outside Parliament after opening a new session in 1942. UPPER RIGHT: Princess Alice in August 1942 with her first cousin, the Dutch Queen Wilhelmina, who had fled Holland in 1940. LOWER LEFT: the Athlones receive another royal exile – King George II of the Hellenes – at Rideau Hall; July 1942. LOWER RIGHT: the Earl in his office at Rideau Hall: the photograph is signed *Alge*, his family nickname. ABOVE: with a ski-ing party at Camp Fortune in January 1943. RIGHT: 'Endless, endless charity work,' Princess Alice described her duties in Canada. Here, in 1943, at the Sun Life Building in Montreal, she looks through magazines and books being packed for Canadian troops in Europe.

OPPOSITE PAGE, TOP LEFT: the Earl of Athlone with President Roosevelt, Winston Churchill and Mr Mackenzie King at Quebec for the first wartime conference, August 1943. TOP RIGHT: Lord Athlone confers an honorary law degree on President Roosevelt at Rideau Hall that month. BOTTOM: the Athlones and Mr Mackenzie King with their Conference guests and their wives at the Citadel. RIGHT: Lord Athlone looks on approvingly as McGill University awards degrees to Roosevelt and Churchill after the second Quebec Conference, in September 1944. BELOW: celebrating the Silver Jubilee of the RCAF at the Officers' Mess in Ottawa, March 1945. BOTTOM: Princess Alice keeping her personal albums up to date at Rideau Hall.

House because that charming family the Athlones is there.' But a meeting did eventually take place, though Princess Alice noted that there was still 'much feeling against Wallis' in Canada.

As the British and Canadian governments were anxious to maintain the Windsors' visit at a low profile, their entry into Canada was arranged, not via Montreal, Ottawa and Winnipeg, but by crossing the US-Canadian border at North Portal, between North Dakota and Saskatchewan. The couple received roars of welcome at Moose Jaw, while at Calgary the density of the crowds was so great that a planned tour of the town had to be cancelled. But the nine-day visit proved not only a long campaign successfully accomplished, but also a most relaxing and fulfilling time. The Duke and Duchess took long, leisurely rambles together; he took himself off duck shooting; she got to know the local people and talked about her child welfare work back in the Bahamas. The Duke fixed a reunion with the Stony Indians who had created him Chief Morning Star nearly a quarter of a century earlier, and received an emotional welcome from them. And when the couple left to return to Nassau, there were huge crowds to see them off at Calgary station, with songs, cheers and handshakes continuing even as the train pulled out.

Meanwhile, the Earl and Countess of Athlone made the most of their own leisure time in Canada. Summer gave them the opportunity to bathe in the lakes around Ottawa, to go for long drives and picnics in the countryside, and to play tennis and badminton. Winter provided the wherewithal to go sleighing in the snow and skating on the ice. They therefore made no complaint about having to stay until the early part of 1946, especially as conditions in austerity-wracked Britain offered no incentive to come home. Indeed, when they did eventually leave Canada, they sailed to Britain via the West Indies, so as, in Princess Alice's discreet words, 'to give the English spring a chance to re-establish itself before we returned home!'

CHAPTER THREE

THE AGE OF ELIZABETH

STAMPEDE AND SQUARE-DANCE: THE LAST EMPIRE TOUR

After the Second World War, as after the first, there was a concerted royal effort to do the Empire rounds again, and the King and Queen, accompanied by their two daughters, began the cycle with a long, colourful and triumphal tour of South Africa in 1947. During it, Princess Elizabeth became of age, dedicating herself to the Empire's service for life, and it was she who was chosen to represent the King when, in 1951, Canada's turn for another royal tour came round. In the twelve years since her parents' visit, the changes were, for the times, remarkable. It was the first major royal tour in which the aeroplane played a part, the outward journey from London and several internal connections being made by air. It was also the first in which televised outside broadcasts allowed those Canadians fortunate enough to possess televisions to see the progress of the visit from time to time. Above all, it was the first in which the celebrity was not the monarch or his eldest son, but a young and attractive princess, accompanied by her sporty, personable and good-looking consort. It all combined to make the visit, despite its slavish similarity to those of past years, sufficiently different and lively for it to be a success pretty well from the start. As if to pay special tribute to their hosts, the royal couple's official portraits to mark the tour were taken by the Ottawa photographer, Karsh, and the Princess took with her the full-length mink coat which the people of Canada had given to her on her marriage four years earlier.

For some time the tour was in the balance owing to the King's severe illness, which, as we now know, signalled the road to his death four months later. As a result, the Princess and the Duke of Edinburgh left England a week behind schedule, carrying with them a draft accession declaration and messages to both British Houses of Parliament in the event of the King's death, and the sea voyage with a ceremonial disembarkation planned at Quebec Harbour had to be substituted for a quick journey by air with muted civilities at Montreal airport. The ill wind blew some good, however, for it was while watching the controls being operated on the royal aircraft during this flight that the Duke of Edinburgh first conceived the desire to fly that prompted him, soon afterwards, to train for the wings he gained two years later.

Appropriately, perhaps, they arrived on Thanksgiving Day, though the drizzling rain that greeted them augured ill for their chances with the weather for the next five weeks.

Indeed, rain became such a persistent feature that, by the time the tour reached Winnipeg, the organisers had persuaded de Havilland to manufacture a plexiglass car-roof so that the royal couple might be protected from the weather, yet still be visible to the huge crowds who stood in appalling conditions to cheer them. Princess Elizabeth, once installed in the newly modified vehicle, was complimented by Prince Philip's private secretary Michael Parker, who thought she looked 'like an orchid wrapped in cellophane'. The car's other practical embellishments to this same end were interior lighting from below, and a back-seat heater - but it wasn't the complete answer to the problems of the climate. At Regina, the first frosts of the tour drove an open-air display by the Mounties indoors, and at a Calgary stampede, seventeen degrees of frost and a blizzard - dismissed contemptuously by the locals as 'just confetti' - had the visitors wrapped in thick electric blankets. And rain soaked the ground so thoroughly at Vancouver that press buses, laden with a total of 150 journalists and photographers, were bogged down, their passengers missing a tree-planting ceremony in which Princess Elizabeth shovelled mud rather than earth onto the sapling's roots. But the royal couple were better prepared for their visit to Niagara Falls: the Duke was fully togged out in black oilskins and rubber boots; the Princess was more elegantly robed in rose-coloured waterproofs.

It is now, and was then, a cliché to talk of adverse weather being incapable of suppressing the popular clamour for royalty, but the truth of that observation was evident during the whole of those hectic five weeks. The 13,000 schoolchildren who sang O Canada at Ottawa in the early days turned out to be a comparatively small crowd. There were 40,000 of them to cheer the visitors to the echo at Toronto, and a civic reception at the City Hall became the occasion for chaotic crowd behaviour in which people in the nearby streets rushed around everywhere for the best view, clambered up outer walls of buildings, shinned up forbidden lamp-posts and statues, and left the emergency services with no fewer than eighty stretcher cases to deal with.

With such an air of informality around them, it was natural that the royal couple should cheerfully tolerate the lèse-majesté of being addressed as Betty and Phil Windsor by the crowds, whose enthusiastic welcome left even the Duke of Edinburgh speechless. 'I cannot hope to put into words what I feel about it,' he said of the city's overwhelming hospitality at a Board of Trade luncheon, 'but I do want to thank everybody for making us feel so much at home.' Hundreds of Indian children gathered at Fort William, having travelled

OPPOSITE: Princess Elizabeth and her husband at their Laurentian Mountains lodge in Sainte-Agathe in 1951.

four hundred miles by canoe from their compounds to see the Princess and her husband. At Montreal, the royal couple made a 25-mile tour of the city's streets by car, passing before an estimated two million people lining the route. From the first week, when all Quebec's church bells sounded their welcoming peals, and when the key to Ottawa was presented to the Princess as representing 'the key to two hundred thousand loyal hearts', neither hosts nor guests could have been in any doubt about the strength of popular feeling for this refreshingly young couple. Less numerous communities more than made up for their lack of numbers by their imaginative enthusiasm. When, for instance, late one night, the royal train stopped at a tiny halt in the Rockies, the Edinburghs stepped out into a blizzard, to the strains of thousands of invisible admirers singing *The Loveliest Night of the Year!*

In return, they were game for most of the delights the Canadians staged for them. They turned up for a square-dance party thrown by the Governor-General in Ottawa, Princess Elizabeth wearing a gingham blouse and swaggering dirndl, while the Duke looked positively rakish in blue jeans, suede loafers, a scarlet necktie and a check shirt that, some said, still had the price tag attached! At Calgary, they arrived, escorted not only by a squad of Mounties but also by contingents of cowboys and Indians, at the Stampede in an old mail-coach - the Halifax, Truro and Pictou - that had ferried the Prince of Wales about in 1860 and still had his feathers emblazoned on the side to prove it. The Duke, wearing a ten-gallon stetson, was in superb spirits after having joined his wife for a cow-puncher's lunch in a chuck-wagon. The grub-pile included sow-belly, punk and axle-grease, CPR strawberries, and sinkers. Or, in King's English, the menu included boiled pork, bread and butter, prunes, and doughnuts. At Edmonton, they watched a football game between the Edmonton Eskimos and the Winnipeg Blue Bombers; at North Bay, Ontario, they met the Dionne quins - now seventeen years old and still world celebrities; and at Victoria, Princess Elizabeth actually drove a locomotive for fifteen miles, with her husband lending an occasional hand. In addition, the Duke discovered that one of his valets shared his predilection for practical jokes, and borrowed, to try out on his wife, several gadgets which the valet had bought from local joke-shops. Stories quickly took root that the heiress to the Throne had opened a small desk-box to find a snake inside it, had been chased along corridors by the Duke wearing a pair of monstrous false teeth, and was for ever wary of devices which might pass on an electric shock when touched.

TOP LEFT: Princess Elizabeth and her husband on the royal train at Montreal, October 1951, on the first stage of their tour. ABOVE: the Princess telephones home for news of the King. BELOW: in Ottawa, the Princess hands over a carpet worked by Queen Mary to the I.O.D.E. OPPOSITE PAGE, ABOVE: the royal visitors at the Governor General's barn-dance at Rideau Hall BELOW: the Princess plants a maple tree in the grounds of Rideau Hall.

There was, of course, for a tour which was to embrace every Canadian province in just thirty-five days, a huge amount of rail travel for the royal couple, undertaken in a ten-coach train whose living quarters were decorated in Princess Elizabeth's favourite colour, sea-green. But the Duke didn't take too kindly to the continual train journeys, and found the heating system particularly overpowering. After one long journey, to Vancouver, he complained philosophically to the Mayor that he felt rather like a poached egg! But it could have been worse. At St Catherine's, near Hamilton, the train driver mistook the beginning of the town's musical farewell to its visitors for a signal to move off. The train trundled down the line, till the mistake was realised, and the red-faced driver had to reverse it to collect his royal passengers. Little else went desperately wrong on the tour - at least until they reached Halifax, where Princess Elizabeth presented a trophy to a Mountie who had won a shooting competition. The champion first dropped the base of the trophy; then, as the Duke stooped to pick it up for him, dropped the trophy itself, complete with lid.

Incidents like these tended to obscure the serious side of the tour, but there are still plaques throughout the whole

ABOVE: stetsons and electric blankets: the Edinburghs enjoying the fun at the Little Calgary Stampede.
LEFT: Princess Elizabeth and her husband arriving at the entrance to the scenic tunnel for the trip to the foot of Niagara Falls.
OPPOSITE PAGE, TOP LEFT: the royal couple with Rear-Admiral Wallace B. Creery on the bridge of the *Crusader*, off Victoria, B.C.
TOP RIGHT: Princess Elizabeth and the Duke of Edinburgh being formally greeted at Stanley Park, Vancouver. The royal car, with its famous plexiglass roof, is in the background.
BOTTOM LEFT: dressed as a cowboy, Mayor McKay of Calgary shows Princess Elizabeth his ten-gallon hat.
BOTTOM RIGHT: Princess and Duke meet Chief and Squaw during a visit to Indian tribes in Alberta.

tapestry carpet, worked by Queen Mary herself, to the National Gallery in Ottawa.

Generally, however, the giving of gifts went the other way, and the royal couple came home with an abundance of presents. Jewellery was, predictably, the favourite - Quebec gave the Princess a jewelled brooch replica of the Quebec Shield, with its panel of fleur-de-lys, while Toronto offered a gold maple leaf brooch encrusted with diamonds. Local offerings revealed a wider range of imaginative variations, including a silver fox cape from Charlottetown, a Christmas tree with 400 ornaments from New Brunswick, a bearskin rug from Edmonton, a cape of breath-of-spring silver-blue mink from the Hudson's Bay Company, in lieu of the black beaver skin traditionally due to royalty, and an enormous cheese from Salmon Arm, near Kamloops. Nor were the Edinburghs' two children forgotten. Toronto gave mechanical toys for them, Windsor presented replicas of cars made by the local Ford Company, Kapuskasing donated a nursery-sized radiogramophone, while at Calgary an Indian squaw called Mrs Heavyshield presented Princess Elizabeth with a doeskin tribal suit for the 14-month-old Princess Anne.

In this respect it was unfortunate that the royal parents could not be back in London in time to celebrate Prince

breadth of the country to prove the more earnest purpose of the royal visit and the tally of no fewer than seventy stops which comprised it. Significantly, the Princess and her husband kept Remembrance Day with the Canadians, laying a wreath at the War Memorial at St John's - just as a month earlier they had placed one at Toronto - in honour of the 42,000 Canadians who had died in an Empire's service during the recent war. The Duke occasionally struck out on his own pet themes, as at a dinner in Toronto, when he praised Canadian scientists and research workers as 'second to none in the world'. For his wife, there were more domestic-orientated duties, including the presentation of a grospoint

Charles' third birthday in mid-November, but such are the disadvantages - and generations of royals and their children have become well accustomed to them - that go hand in hand with the privilege of monumental journeys of lifetimes. By the time this one was all over, the Princess and her husband had covered over 15,000 miles in the now customary five-week schedule. Prince Philip's official biographer described the journey graphically and aptly as 'studded with stops, like suckers on an octopus.' It offered only brief respites, like the three-day shooting holiday at a wooden lodge at Eagle's Crest on Vancouver Island, a snowbound weekend at Quebec, and a boat-trip in the Strait of Georgia in which, despite teeming rain and a dangerously heavy swell, the royal couple caught eight young salmon which they triumphantly cooked for lunch.

All in all, both were mightily impressed by Canada. Prince Philip, in particular, found the adventurous, try-anything-once nature of many Canadians refreshing, and he emphasised the country's evident maturity. 'Canada is wrong,' he remarked, 'in insisting that it is a young country. Youth means inexperience and lack of judgement. I do not see how this description can fit a nation that pushed a railway line through the Rockies, developed the prairies, exploited the vast natural resources of timber, oil and water power, and is steadily pushing the last frontier forward.' Princess Elizabeth, too, was full of enthusiasm - though she did confess that she was hardly able to take in the remorseless succession of novel and fascinating experiences - when she spoke of her travels at the

54

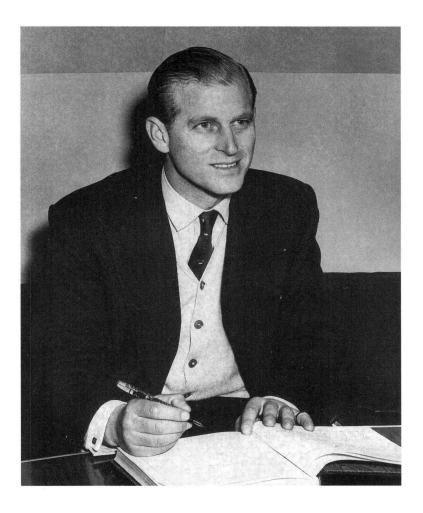

OPPOSITE PAGE, TOP: Princess Elizabeth driving the royal train *en route* for Edmonton: the Duke acted as fireman. BOTTOM: the Princess meets the Dionne quins at North Bay on the way to Montreal. ABOVE LEFT: the royal couple broke their Canadian tour for a few days in the U.S. in early November. Here, the Duke signs the guest log of the R.C.A.F. plane that flew them back to Montreal.

ABOVE RIGHT: the royal visitors at Fort William, Ontario, inspecting a basket woven by Indians. BELOW LEFT: being escorted to their hotel in Fredericton by New Brunswick's Premier McLaren. BELOW: large crowds at Sainte-Agathe in the snow-covered Laurentians, as the Princess and her husband attended Sunday service at Trinity Anglican church.

Guildhall upon her return to London. Like her grandfather fifty years earlier, she hoped that 'people from the United Kingdom will go out and make their life beside the fine men and women who form the nation of Canada', a country which, she continued, 'is on its way to becoming one of the greatest in the world' and for which 'its people have placed in our hearts a love which will never grow cold, and which will always draw us back to her shores.'

Ten weeks later, she became Canada's sovereign.

BELOW, LEFT: the Princess and Duke at Halifax's Dalhousie University. BELOW: at St. John's, after wreath-laying at the War Memorial. CENTRE LEFT: a brief stop at Truro, N.S. BOTTOM RIGHT: on the balcony of the Parliament buildings, Charlottetown. BOTTOM LEFT: a farewell inspection of HMCS *Ontario*'s crew. OPPOSITE: October 1957. With John Diefenbaker at the start of her first visit as Queen, Elizabeth II at Uplands Airport, Ottawa.

'HAPPY TO BE BACK': THE QUEEN CLAIMS HER CANADA

It was six years before the Queen returned to the land which, at the end of that first tour, she had described as 'a country that has become a second home in every sense', and which, as if to justify that description, she has visited no fewer than sixteen times in the course of her reign to date. Despite the long and eventful interval in between, she well remembered her last, lingering look at the Maritime Provinces as, pitching and pulling against the swell, her ship sailed away in November 1951. 'When my husband and I were leaving Canada last time, in the teeth of a gale,' she told her hosts on the first day of her 1957 tour, 'we heard kindly people at Portugal Cove singing *Will Ye No' Come Back Again?* Now, after six years, I want you to know how happy I am to be in Canada once again.'

ABOVE: the Queen meets the Diefenbakers on arrival at the Château Laurier for a government reception. LEFT: the Queen and the Duke of Edinburgh in the Senate Chamber during the Opening of Parliament ceremony. ABOVE, LEFT: the procession leaving the Chamber afterwards. OPPOSITE PAGE, TOP LEFT: the Queen and Duke stand under the arch of the Peace Tower to receive the Royal Salute and BOTTOM LEFT, in full State dress, leaving the Parliament Buildings in an open car. TOP RIGHT: the Queen chairs a Canadian Privy Council meeting at Canada House, Ottawa on October 17, 1957. BOTTOM RIGHT: the royal visitors with Governor-General Massey at Government House, Ottawa.

That sentiment might at this distance of time seemed no more than platitudinous, but it was in all probability infinitely more genuine than many may have suspected. To her, the visit represented something of an escape from a Britain then awash with rumours about the state of her marriage, as well as some pretty incisive criticism of the monarchy and herself. Lord Altrincham had only that summer claimed that 'the personality conveyed by the utterances put into her mouth is that of a priggish schoolgirl'; the playwright John Osborne had described the monarchy as 'the gold filling in the mouth of decay', and had questioned the political value and moral stimulus of 'the royal round of gracious boredom, the protocol of ancient fatuity.' Meanwhile, Malcolm Muggeridge weighed in by taking a tilt at the Queen's 'dowdy, frumpish' appearance and 'banal' behaviour. The Queen seemed unable, at the very beginning of her 1957 tour, to leave the flak entirely behind her, for even as she arrived in Canada, a public opinion survey conducted just beforehand showed a marked public indifference to the event - a reaction, no doubt, to the

enormous enthusiasm orchestrated at the time of the Coronation and sustained for too long afterwards.

It was therefore all the more surprising, and certainly gratifying, that hundreds of thousands of people flocked to Ottawa to give as rapturous a start to this tour as any in the Queen's experience, before or since, a reception which gave the programme an initial momentum which, despite its unoriginal format, it was not to lose. The tour became particularly famous for the fact that it incorporated the first televised broadcast ever made by the Queen - something of a trial run, one felt, for the Christmas broadcast due to be screened back in Britain later that year - which was accomplished only after several long and anxious rehearsals. This was also the tour in which, at the request of Prime Minister John Diefenbaker, Prince Philip was made a Canadian Privy Counsellor, and in which the Queen became the first reigning sovereign to open the Canadian Parliament in person - 'a splendid occasion,' Prince Philip later declared it, 'and something to which the Queen had long been looking

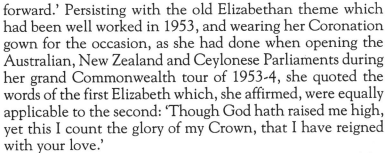

forward.' Persisting with the old Elizabethan theme which had been well worked in 1953, and wearing her Coronation gown for the occasion, as she had done when opening the Australian, New Zealand and Ceylonese Parliaments during her grand Commonwealth tour of 1953-4, she quoted the words of the first Elizabeth which, she affirmed, were equally applicable to the second: 'Though God hath raised me high, yet this I count the glory of my Crown, that I have reigned with your love.'

The occasion proved more symbolic still. Conscious of the rarity of major royal visits to Canada during the century, the Queen left her Canadian subjects in no doubt as to their equality with the British as far as her constitutional role was concerned. 'I greet you as your Queen,' she stressed during her speech from the Throne. 'Together we constitute the Parliament of Canada.' She went even further when, at the end of her tour, she left for a brief visit to the United States. In her final major speech in Canada beforehand, she emphasised that she would 'be going as Head of the Canadian

nation to pay a State Visit to our great neighbouring country. When you have read about the events in Washington and other places, I want you to reflect that it is the Queen of Canada and her husband who are concerned in them.'

By the most recent standards, this was a comparatively staid tour, but it did have its moments of unrehearsed excitement and humour. Only five minutes before the ceremony of the State Opening of Parliament was due to begin, all the lights in the chamber fused because the film lighting requirements had overloaded the system. A whole army of electricians were forced to beaver away to get things back to normal again before the Queen and Duke of Edinburgh arrived. They succeeded and, according to one calculation, with a full 55 seconds to spare! Then there was the meeting in Ontario between the Duke and the Chief of the Six Nations tribe. The Chief wore regular Western dress, and the absence of traditional Indian garb left the Duke with no conversation opener. With his eagle eye, however, the Duke did spot a button-badge on the Chief's lapel, and with some

ABOVE: beginning their 1959 tour, the Queen and Prince Philip visited the Bowater Paper Mill in Newfoundland. BELOW: a relaxed and happy royal couple being driven along Montreal's St James's Street. BELOW RIGHT: 'Which of you is the eldest?' the Queen asked the Hargreaves quads during her visit to Sault Ste-Marie, Ontario. OPPOSITE PAGE, TOP LEFT: the Queen with Mr Diefenbaker after she had unveiled this impressive Commonwealth Air Forces memorial in Ottawa. TOP RIGHT: the Queen with Mrs Savignac on board the Royal Yacht *Britannia* at Montreal, shortly before the opening of the St Lawrence Seaway. BOTTOM LEFT: the Queen and Prince Philip arriving for a ceremony to present new colours to army units on Parliament Hill, Ottawa. BOTTOM RIGHT: the Queen with former villagers of Long Sault, flooded in the construction of the St Lawrence Seaway.

relief dutifully enquired, 'What's the significance?' 'Twenty-five years with the Post Office,' came the nonchalant reply!

Though Prince Philip since described the tour appreciatively as 'blessed with glorious weather and beautiful colours,' its whole character paled by contrast with one that he had made in the summer of 1954. This visit, with as its primary purpose the opening of the Empire Games at Vancouver, which the Duke had two years previously promised to perform, developed into a 20-day tour of the type for which he has become famous and which admirably suits his questing, adventurous and largely informal nature. In basic terms it became a fact-finding trip to see Canadians at work, to share the discoveries of the potential of the great north-west in particular, and to learn more about new pioneering industries. In the interests of saving time, much of the Duke's travelling was done by air, and the casual character of the tour was maintained by outlawing all unnecessary protocol. The emphasis on new industry and emergent technology at a time when these two factors were of prime importance in Canada's economic and social development, was unending. The Duke toured an atomic plant at Chalk River, visited the British Columbian backwoods, where the town of Kitimat had sprouted up around a new aluminium smelting plant, toured Fort Radium - then the world's second largest source of radium, and inspected gold-mines at Yellowknife. And it was from Yellowknife that he broadcast his confession that, above all else, the tour was satisfying a long-held ambition to see Canada for himself. This aim, conceived when, as a boy, he read of Canada's north-west regions, had received added impetus from parts of the 1951 royal visit. Now he was happy that 'everything I have seen confirms my belief that Canada is on the threshold of an era of great prosperity.'

In between whiles, the old Canada was not forgotten. The Duke visited, for instance, the cabin of Dan McGraw at Whitehorse, in the Yukon, and the old Hudson's Bay Company headquarters at Fort Simpson, and he met Jim Koiyakok, then

ABOVE: the Queen presenting new colours to the Canadian Argyll and Sutherland Highlanders in Ottawa. ABOVE RIGHT: After having jointly opened the St Lawrence Seaway, the Queen and President Eisenhower drove from Lambert Lock to join the Royal Yacht *Britannia* for a short trip along the Seaway. BELOW LEFT: 'Handsome, dashing, even debonair,' was how they described Prince Philip after this photograph was taken at a dinner-dance at Montreal's Queen Elizabeth Hotel, where BELOW RIGHT he danced with Mrs Fournier, wife of the city's Lord Mayor. OPPOSITE PAGE: another visit to Calgary, with the royal couple in animated mood at the annual July Stampede.

With the advent of militant separatism, the Queen's 1964 tour was notably more tense than any others before or since, but the Queen put a brave face on things as LEFT she arrived at RCAF Base Summerside to begin her visit to Charlottetown that October. OPPOSITE PAGE, BOTTOM: ten-year-old Terry Leclair, handicapped by polio, presents the official bouquet to the Queen in Charlottetown, watched by the Duke of Edinburgh, Mr and Mrs Lester Pearson, and (behind) Governor-General Georges Vanier. OPPOSITE PAGE, TOP: the Queen is even more relaxed as she meets the cast of the Royal Variety Performance at the city's Confederation Memorial Theatre. Lorne Green, the famous *Bonanza* celebrity is chatting with Prince Philip as Prime Minister Lester Pearson (background) looks on. After the performance, the Queen and her husband show no sign of anxiety as they leave Charlottetown on board the Royal Yacht BOTTOM LEFT for the next stage of the eight-day tour – Quebec.

the most renowned Inuit hunter in the Arctic. Novel experiences included travelling in an amphibious plane at Fort Nelson, visiting Great Bear Lake - where the Duke stayed in a simple clapboard guest-house which was almost lost in the surrounding immensity, and crossing the Arctic Circle, an achievement which not only made him the first member of the Royal Family to do so, but also earned for him the title 'Airborne Iceworm of the Initial Degree.' There were breathlessly superb views of the Rockies blanketed with snow, barbecues on the beaches of frozen lakes, swimming in the comparative warmth of Vancouver, and an idiosyncratic trip aboard a paddle steamer up the Yukon River to the strains of *Cruisin' Down the River on a Sunday Afternoon*. The Duke found the opportunity to relive this gesture of slight eccentricity at Churchill: here he learned that the children of the 200-house settlement had been promised something special, so he dressed up in his uniform of Field Marshal of the Royal Air Force and drove through the town in an open jeep! For their part, the Canadians knew no bounds in their generosity. By the end of August the Duke was back in London bearing all manner of gifts for his children - two polar bear skins, an Arctic trapper's kit, Indian tunics, Inuit sledges - as well as advice, should it ever be needed, on how to live off caribou, Arctic trout, moose-meat and bison sandwiches!

There can be little doubt that the rewards the Duke gleaned from this solo tour influenced the character of the second visit which he and his wife undertook as Queen and Consort in 1959, when the emphasis was on the need to visit many outlying districts never before visited by royalty. There

was a cruise through the islands of Ontario's Georgian Bay and on Lake Huron and a high-summer train journey through the Rockies; there were visits to Deer Lake in Newfoundland, to Arvida - way up the Sanguenay on Lake St John - to the gold rush area of the Klondike and to the Northwest Territories towns of Yellowknife and Uranium City; there were tours of aluminium-smelting plants, of iron workings in Labrador, of nickel mines near Sudbury. The royal couple cheerfully bumped along thirty miles of dusty road to inspect a paper mill; travelled on a narrow-gauge railway from Whitehorse to McCrea in a train built seventy years earlier to transport armies of gold prospectors to the area; were invited into pre-fabricated homes in Schefferville, Quebec, and to workers' homes at Harmon Airbase; and met fur-trappers, fishermen and lumberjacks. 'A wonderful experience,' the Queen summed up; 'strenuous but intensely interesting.'

In the course of that experience, they journeyed by BOAC aircraft, the Royal Yacht, cars, an assortment of smaller aircraft, seaplanes, boats, royal barge and royal train. Their train was eight coaches long, and steamed over both Canadian

RIGHT: in Quebec, General Vanier offers the Queen a volume of the regimental history of the Royal 22nd Regiment. BELOW: in Ottawa, Lester Pearson presents an amphibious car to the royal couple.

National and Canadian Pacific track, disposing of and collecting laundry at Calgary, Kamloops, Vancouver and Edmonton three times a week. Diplomatic boxes were delivered onto it by courier service from Royal Canadian Air Force pilots in either jet planes or what were then known as conventional aircraft. Of the eight coaches, the Queen and Prince Philip had a coach to themselves; four coaches contained their travelling household, which included six footmen, the Queen's hairdresser and her page; one accommodated the office and living quarters of her Private Secretary; and one housed thirteen members of the Royal Canadian Mounted Police. The remaining coach was given over to the secretary of the programme committee, whose job was to ensure the royal schedule was adhered to and all appropriate arrangements made or suitably amended as the tour progressed. It also served as a communications centre complete with letter boxes said to be 'under the control of the confidential clerk who will co-ordinate mail arrangements.'

Some of the more urban parts of the tour were no less gruelling than those to wilder districts. A thirty-mile motor

LEFT: as fighting erupts outside, the Queen speaks to her hosts in Quebec's Parliament Buildings.

BELOW: the Queen and Prince Philip arriving at the Château Frontenac in Quebec for a State dinner.

tour of Montreal's streets took place in boiling hot weather, while the freezing fog which greeted the Queen in Newfoundland contrasted dramatically with the 90-degree heat of Toronto where she was on duty fourteen hours a day. And at a Montreal ball, she and Prince Philip were forced to leave early because, as soon as they took the floor, everyone else who could crowded onto it, leaving no latitude for dancing; while those who couldn't climbed onto chairs and tables, careless of the crash of cutlery and crockery around them, to get a better view of what were, in events, fairly static proceedings. Officials watched helplessly as the chaos was compounded, horrified that, in the remarkably restrained words of one of the them, 'the ordinary rules of behaviour were forgotten.'

The catalyst for the visit was the ceremonial opening of the St Lawrence Seaway, which the Queen performed in conjunction with President Eisenhower before taking a leisurely five-hour passage along it to the accompanying peal of riverside church bells, the blast of saluting cannon and the whistles and sirens of passing rivercraft. The tour also provided Prince Philip with the customary chance, which he rarely passes up, of transmitting his own personal interpretation of life to the average Canadian. At Toronto, for instance, he praised his hosts' achievements by stating that 'there is hardly any field of science, engineering and technology in which

OPPOSITE PAGE, TOP LEFT: the Queen in *Expo 67*'s British Pavilion at Montreal. TOP RIGHT: Prince Philip speaking at a Government House garden party in Quebec. BOTTOM: the Queen with her 1967 Canadian Cabinet. THIS PAGE, RIGHT: with the Prime Minister, the royal couple watch a centennial fireworks display, Nepean Point. BELOW: with young Canadians at a dinner at Government House.

Canada cannot show some outstanding example.' Yet, on the other hand, when the Canadian Medical Association invited him to address them as their President, he warned of the increasing pressure of urban life on mental and physical health and ventured the opinion that Canada's achievements in sport were 'hardly in keeping with a country which claims almost the highest standard of living in the world.'

But perhaps the visit will best be remembered for the discovery - admittedly just after its completion - that the Queen was then in the early stages of her third pregnancy. Although journalists had noted that, on their arrival in the country, Prince Philip looked 'subdued, in contrast to his wife's higher spirits', it was soon to be the Queen who looked increasingly off-colour as the tour continued. The strain began to tell forcibly during the western leg of the programme, though even when she missed a visit to Dawson City, the official explanation of her indisposition was given as 'a stomach upset and fatigue.' Later, 'better, but not fully recovered', as the Palace discreetly warned, she completed a whistle-stop tour of fifteen townships on her journey eastwards before the final round of duties in the Maritime Provinces. It was not until she arrived back in Britain that the news of her pregnancy was released, and it is appropriate that Prince Andrew, the child born to her the following February, should have been so closely associated with Canada both before and after his marriage.

The Queen's 1970 tour. TOP RIGHT: the Queen and Mr Trudeau examine Eskimo harpoons, Frobisher Bay. RIGHT: a beaver, one of two representing Hudson's Bay rental, peeks out of his box as Lord Amory presents them to the Queen, Lower Fort Garry. BELOW: the Queen in the Company's 'Northern Stores' replica of a 1600s trading post. BELOW RIGHT: checking out a canoe later used in the Fort Providence to Inuvik centennial race.

SOUL-SEARCHING AND SEPARATISM: THE CROWN UNDER QUESTION

The questioning social mood of the Sixties involved Canada as much as any other western country, and the issue here which raised most questions - and no little acrimony - during that decade, was that of Quebec. Signs of its delicate nature surfaced during a month-long trip to Canada undertaken by the Duke of Edinburgh in May 1962 - mainly on business, but also comprising a three-day break at the E.P. Taylor ranch and a five-day fishing holiday in Quebec province - when, at a general press conference, he found himself having to field, with great diplomacy, unexpected questions fired at him regarding the emergent separatist tendencies among Quebec's Francophone communities. But it was the Queen who took the full force of the increasingly bitter debate when, two years later, she visited Quebec as part of a short tour which also took in Ottawa and Charlottetown in celebration of the centenary of the visits of the Fathers of the Confederation. No sooner had the Queen's prospective visit been announced than the Quebec separatists rose up in hot protest, resolved, in the words of their leader Marcel Chaput, 'to let her know brutally that she is not welcome in Quebec or French Canada.' He made veiled references to the possibility of assassination, which others less restrained than he developed into explicit threats, and the dire possibilities burgeoned so oppressively that the tour itself became something of a blueprint for the intense security that has surrounded the Queen ever since.

Thus she arrived at Charlottetown, Prince Edward Island, to be welcomed in a steel enclosure surrounded by barbed wire, and with massive barricades erected everywhere. The only light-hearted moment seemed to be the strange absence of the letter C on the neon banner which was meant to read 'Welcome to Charlottetown'! Meanwhile, police were roaming the streets of Quebec, almost hungry for victims, on what was to become known as 'the day of the cudgel'. In the event, all protest took place without violence, and the Queen and Prince Philip were subjected to nothing more injurious than the turned backs of thousands of separatists who lined the royal route through the city, and the virulently anti-monarchist sentiments of scores of hostile posters. From that tour, which she had long been urged to cancel or postpone for her own safety, the Queen emerged almost a heroine, the subject of praiseworthy comparisons with the most dutiful and determined of her ancestors, the bold and gritty mother of four who defied the menaces of a dangerous and unpredictable foe.

The 1964 experience did not prevent the Queen from returning to Canada three years later, in order to celebrate the centenary of the Confederation and to tour *Expo 67*. As might have been expected in this, the proudest of all years for

Canadians, this short summer visit was full of celebration, and the Queen experienced the best of it. She presented no fewer than six new regimental Colours in a spectacular ceremony on Parliament Hill, was greeted with a 'Royal Hullaballoo' during a programme of fun and entertainment at Lansdowne Park, attended a magnificent firework display at Nepean, and swore in nine provincial premiers amid the traditionally solemn proceedings of a Canadian Privy Council meeting. Of course, the weather did its usual trick when the Queen spent her first day in Montreal to visit the Exposition, and much of the tour was carried out under her famous black umbrella. But, though it compared badly with the beautifully sunlit day the previous April on which Prime Minister Lester Pearson had lit the inaugural torch in the Place des Nations, it did not spoil the success of the Queen's visit.

Meanwhile, the separatist argument continued, fired in particular by the French President de Gaulle when, on a visit to the province in the late 1960s, he uttered his famous public prayer: *Vive le Québec Libre*. It raised itself again during the Queen's Silver Jubilee visit to Canada when, despite some placatory words about the relevance of monarchy from Prince Philip in 1969, the French-speaking community collided with the federal government over the role of the Crown in Canada. Heavy debate deteriorated into such naked

BOTTOM LEFT: Haida Indians dance for the royals at Sandspit, B.C. in 1971. BELOW: royal curtseys at New Westminster's 1971 May festival. BOTTOM: the captain of Hyack Anvil Battery explains the New Westminster Anvil Salute process to the Queen.

LEFT: The Queen swamped by crowds at the C.N.E. Grounds in Toronto, June 1973, and BOTTOM in the city's Nathan Phillips Square. BELOW LEFT: accepting the gift of a horse at the RCMP Training Depot, Regina. BELOW: the Queen and Prince Philip in earnest conversation during an Indian dance at Calgary. OPPOSITE PAGE, TOP LEFT: an Indian girl grins after giving the Queen a bouquet at Newcastle, N.B. during her 1976 tour. TOP RIGHT: the Queen with Brownies at Wolfville, N.S. BOTTOM: prior to her 1976 visit, the Queen received Canadian Indian Chiefs and their wives at Buckingham Palace.

partisanship that, within days before the Queen's visit in October 1977, a whole consignment of Silver Jubilee memorabilia had to be destroyed because it bore English wording only, rather than English and French. The separatists' new leader, René Levesque, worked a calculated slight to the Queen by standing in the receiving line to meet her at a formal reception, with a lighted cigarette butt clutched between his fingers. Prince Philip took the bull by the horns at a dinner party given by Prime Minister Trudeau and discussed the issue of separatism with M. Levesque, who would only say afterwards, 'We disagreed, but subtly'. The Queen, restricted as always by protocol, could only sound a more obviously hopeful note when she addressed the Canadian people on television. 'The Canadian experience has been to illustrate that man's finer instincts can prevail,' she said pointedly. 'My prayer is that you will continue to offer that message to mankind'.

Back in Canada the next year to open the Commonwealth Games at Edmonton - 'You could have heard the cheers from Edmonton to Windsor,' one journalist said of the reception accorded to her - the Queen returned to the same theme, though she must by then have despaired of the state of

relations between English- and French-speaking communities exactly seventy years after her grandfather had pronounced them in such good order. Much of the trouble represented legacies from previous years, but in 1978 the separatists had a new grudge - that Prime Minister Trudeau might use the Queen's visit to flaunt his belief in the value of the British monarchy as presiding head of a fully federated Canada. A carefully-worded speech made by the Queen - partly in

French - at St John's was translated rather too freely into pro-English sentiments, and became an immediate focus for the separatists' new protests. The matter gained such significance that the Queen herself felt obliged to put the record straight in a later speech at Regina, where she emphasised the need to draw different ethnic cultures together, rather than allowing them to flourish in isolation, or in indifference or opposition to each other. 'A free society has to be built on the co-operation and consent of all its people,' she explained, 'free to enjoy and to foster the heritage of their forefathers, but at the same time willing to contribute to a distinctive Canadian culture.'

Unhappily, there was no resolution of this issue even by the time of the Queen's next visit in 1982 - the hastily arranged, five-day stay in Ottawa to sign the Act to patriate the Constitution. There was much celebration of this long-awaited totality of independence after 115 years of diminishing reliance on Britain for foreign policy decisions. Mr Trudeau was jubilant - 'The end of a long winter; the beginning of a new spring,' he proclaimed - but his arch-rival, M. Levesque, was unconvinced. 'It's crazy for the Queen to come here,' he protested. 'We refuse to accept her bringing our symbolic independence' - and he boycotted the signing ceremony, spending the day organising half a dozen meetings in Montreal and Quebec, whipping up the antipathy of the Inuit communities who themselves had grievances over territorial claims, and encouraging all French-speaking citizens to reject the deal. The Queen faced matters squarely when she spoke at the ceremony. Referring to 'the differences and rivalries which have been part of Canada's history, and will probably always exist in such a vast and vigorous land,' she continued: 'Although we regret the absence of its Premier, it is right to associate the people of Quebec with this celebration because without them, Canada would not be what she is today.'

These pious words fell on deaf ears in Quebec, and although the extremism associated with the separatist movement was never to be repeated, it was a full five years before the circumstances were propitious for the Queen to return to the city which bore so many grudges and harboured so much ill-feeling out of the tangle of historical developments from which Canada was desperately trying to escape.

The Queen's Silver Jubilee Tour of 1977. TOP: with Prime Minister Trudeau and the Duke at a gala concert, National Arts Centre, Ottawa. ABOVE: with Roman Catholic and Jewish leaders at an inter-faith service on Parliament Hill. LEFT: opening the 3rd session of the 30th Parliament. OPPOSITE PAGE, TOP LEFT: the Queen accepts a baton holding her speech to open the 1978 Commonwealth Games at Edmonton. TOP RIGHT: hard ground gives the Queen problems at a sod-turning ceremony at Grande Prairie Hospital site, Alberta. BOTTOM: Prince Philip speaking in Winnipeg, on accepting a 1978 International Award for health care.

CHAPTER FOUR

A FAMILY AFFAIR

'STRAWBERRIES ON EVEREST': PRINCE PHILIP WEIGHS IN

By then of course Canadians were becoming used to hosting not just the Queen but also every other member of her growing family. It may come as something of a surprise that since her Accession almost eighty official royal visits have been undertaken in Canada, quite apart from the many strictly private holidays and excursions that the Royal Family have enjoyed here. Prince Philip has been responsible for almost a quarter of such visits on his own account - three times to open games meetings, four to arrange or open Commonwealth Study Conference meetings, most of the remainder in connection with his Award scheme, various regimental obligations, the English Speaking Union and what is now termed the World Wide Fund for Nature. Indeed one of his earliest speeches on conservation was delivered at the Canadian Audubon Society's dinner in Toronto in November 1967, when in his crisp and direct way he pleaded for co-operation between farmers, land reclaimers, irrigation commissioners, foresters, mineral developers, power engineers and planners - who may never have realised what a vital part they were all to play in the forthcoming fight to preserve and improve ecosystems. While giving technological progress its dues - 'I daresay we could grow strawberries on the top of Mount Everest if we really tried' - he could not emphasise strongly enough that humanity's needs should be harnessed 'so that we make no further demands on land resources', and that 'it is really a case of now or never. If we don't get the answer right now, there won't be a second chance'.

Even though it has taken years for the message to get through, the Duke's comments on that particular occasion caused considerable reaction among many of the groups he had singled out, who were convinced they could not possibly be at fault. But in terms of sheer controversy, the tour was as nothing compared with the repercussions of his Autumn 1969 visit - a three-week tour stretching from Ottawa to Vancouver, designed primarily to encourage progress with the Award scheme. This of all his visits to Canada will be remembered as the great foot-in-mouth expedition when the Duke seemed rarely to be out of the news for what he said as opposed to what he did. 'Not another one,' he protested when, as always, his hosts at Calgary gave him a souvenir stetson. Immediate offence. 'I declare this thing open, whatever it is,' he said when opening a new annexe to Vancouver City Hall. More raised eyebrows and crushed pride. At Toronto he made some remark, presumably intended to be a jokey reflection on the media's preoccupation with the monarchy, about the possibility of dressing up the Queen's annual Christmas broadcast and calling it 'The Queen Show'. Shock waves throughout Canada, the USA and Britain.

But the biggest issue of all found expression during a press conference in Ottawa. That same disrespect for the monarchy which had accompanied the push for Quebec separation had by now infected the progressive, free-thinking young, and a question about the current relevance of the Crown in Canada was put to the Duke during his tour. It clearly irritated him and he responded with some asperity in the form of an assurance that 'we don't come here for our health.' The remark hardly endeared him to the Canadians but, in the long term, put them on the spot and forced them to consider how relevant the Crown really was to them. 'If, at any stage,' he went on, 'people feel the monarchy has no further part to play, then for goodness' sake let's end the thing on amicable terms without having a row about it.' Then, on his way back home, he stopped in Washington and gave another press conference in which he pulled the whole issue of royal finances into the political arena, with his almost casual comments about the monarchy 'going into the red next year, I believe.' Certainly, by the time he reached Britain, that particular Canadian tour had become one of the most famous in royal history.

BRINGING THE CHILDREN: A NEW DEPARTURE

The combination of controversies took some time to die down, and the process was without doubt greatly helped by the popular attention being paid to the younger generation of the Royal Family, who had only just begun to play a prominent

OPPOSITE: Prince Philip addresses the Royal Agricultural Society at Toronto's Royal York Hotel in 1967.

part in public life. Canadians will remember with great pleasure the eventful and refreshingly informal programme assigned to Prince Charles and Princess Anne when, for the first time, they accompanied the Queen and Prince Philip to Canada. The year was 1970, the occasion the centenary celebrations of the Northwest Territories and Manitoba. Prince Charles enjoyed his own independent schedule which took him to Ottawa for a couple of days before joining his

ABOVE: the Duke of Edinburgh meeting Chief Patsy Henderson and his wife at Whitehorse, Yukon, in 1954. OPPOSITE PAGE: CENTRE LEFT: inspecting pitchblende ore at a uranium mine at Fort Radium during the same tour. CENTRE RIGHT: chatting with U.S. representatives of the English-Speaking Union at the Château Laurier, Ottawa in 1958. TOP PICTURES: taking part in a televised panel discussion on Commonwealth matters, in Toronto in 1960. BOTTOM: spotting a veteran's loyal tie after taking the Salute at the trooping of colours of the battalions of all three Royal Canadian Regiments of which the Prince is Colonel-in-Chief: London, Ontario, May 1962.

parents and sister on a tour which included demonstrations of gold-panning at Churchill and a Scout jamboree at Camp Nanook, a visit to the Manitoba Derby at Winnipeg, where the Queen presented a silver plate to winning jockey Ron Turcotte, and a game of football between the Winnipeg Blue Bombers and the Saskatchewan Roughriders. During the Yellowknife stage of the tour, the Queen presented a baton containing her message for the forthcoming Commonwealth Games to be held that year in Edinburgh, and it began its four thousand mile journey to the Scottish capital on that day.

The royal visitors called in at St Pierre to hear from the French community there, and the Queen spoke of the open-mindedness of the people which, together with the healthy climate, offered the key to a promising future for Franco-Manitobans. At Benard, they met the Huttentes, a highly religious farming community distinguishable by the plain garb of the menfolk and the long dresses and headscarves worn by their women. An even more fascinating meeting took place at Winnipeg when, during the centenary celebrations in the Legislature grounds, a 100-year-old man told the royals how he had been crippled at the age of six when he was run over by a Red River ox-cart! Meanwhile, more traditionally, the Queen received two beavers from Viscount Amory, the governor of the Hudson's Bay Company, as part of the time-honoured rental payments due, under the 1670 Charter, to the sovereign whenever she visits the Canadian mid-West.

The tour was not without its slight mishaps, of course. Princess Anne, never an easy mover in the then fashionable mini-skirt and stump heels, slipped on a rainsoaked wooden platform staircase at The Pas and very nearly fell several feet. A military display at Camp Shilo was nearly ruined when a helicopter landed too close to the royal dais and threw showers of sand, dirt and rain towards the Queen and her family, who dived behind their umbrellas for shelter. And on another occasion, Prince Charles' helicopter broke down and a spare transport had to be despatched to pick him up to join the Queen.

But for all that, the royal juniors found their Canadian experience something of an eye-opener. Princess Anne toured what must be one of the most northerly golf-courses in the world, at Wasagaming, and visited the Metis Indians. Prince Charles' schedule, appropriately enough, included a visit to Fort Prince of Wales in Manitoba, and to Norway House in the north of the province, where he received a gift of moose hides, before catching up with the rest of the family at Swan River for an outdoor barbecue. And perhaps the nicest thing that happened to him occurred at Brandon when, as his train pulled away at the end of his visit, a man ran out of the crowd and threw the Welsh flag towards him. Appreciatively, the Prince draped it over the edge of the observation platform. The Arctic experience, from Frobisher Bay in Labrador to the Elizabeth Islands, was little short of thrilling in its novelty. The Prince travelled by transports ancient and modern - from dog sleds to snowmobiles - and was treated to an Arctic picnic which included musk ox stew. In the extreme northerly Grise Fjord the severity of the frost compelled him to dress from head to foot in caribou fur. His reaction was typically lighthearted. 'I hope we don't meet a polar bear,' he said. 'He might think I'm in season!'

A family on tour in 1970. OPPOSITE PAGE: the Queen and Princess Anne with Thomasina Emoralik at an Inuit settlement near Resolute Bay. RIGHT: Prince Charles and Prince Philip are surrounded by a sea of Wolf Cubs and Boy Scouts at a Churchill, Manitoba Scout Jamboree. BELOW: Prince Charles serving himself at an outdoor barbecue at Norway House, Manitoba. BELOW RIGHT: an Inuit lady takes the floor in a drum dance, to the delight of Prince Philip and Princess Anne, during the Royal Family's visit to Tuktoyaktuk, on the Beaufort Sea. BOTTOM RIGHT: the Royals hold on to their hats as a helicopter lands near them and showers them with mud splashes and rain during a display at a military base at Shilo, Manitoba.

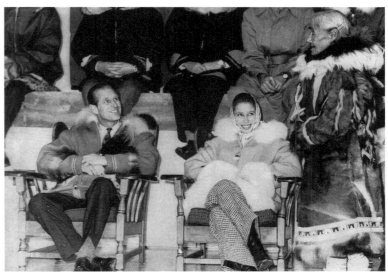

GETTING TO KNOW YOU: A FUTURE KING FOR CANADA

It was almost five years before Prince Charles came to Canada again. Since his 1970 visit, he had been engaged in his service career, primarily with the Royal Navy, and although he had been able to undertake as many as nineteen fairly brief official engagements outside Britain during that time, it was not until the aircraft carrier HMS *Hermes* commenced a programme of NATO excercises in the Atlantic in April 1975 that he was able to strike out for Canadian shores once again. He visited Ottawa for three days before making for the Northwest Territories, sampling life in some of the ice- and snow-bound regions which he had missed on his previous visit. A hardy contingent of pressmen, anticipating news value in the informal, almost fun-filled royal schedule set in its location of Arctic wastes, went with him, and he virtually performed for them. At Resolution Bay's underwater research station he was kitted out in a bright orange diving suit (under which were several layers of woollens), weighted with lead, and loaded with two tanks of oxygen, before taking an exploratory dive beneath the polar ice with a young marine scientist, Dr Joe MacInnes. The Prince spent a full half-hour there, in a temperature of only 28°F, and virtually trapped between six feet of surface ice and the sea bed only thirty feet below. He was in superb sorts when he eventually surfaced, rewarding the waiting photographers' patience and stamina by inflating his diving suit with compressed air and wandering about like some huge, helpless, stranded sea creature. It was a pity that another attempt at levity - the breezy statement that 'I'm off to rub a few noses' - backfired by offending the Eskimos he was about to visit. But he came back in one piece, revelling in stories of how he had been dog-sleighing, husky-trekking and had taken his first meal at which blubber was on the menu!

Before leaving Canada, Prince Charles underwent a four-week helicopter training course with the RCAF at Blissville in New Brunswick, which proved uncomfortably realistic, involving as it did a full fortnight under canvas in unseasonably frosty temperatures - even for the Maritime Provinces. The happy and healthy relationship he had struck up with the press in the north continued here, and he gave several interviews before television film cameras while at the same time making no secret of the fact that, for the first time, he was growing a full set of whiskers. During the fairly lengthy growing stage he took part in a privately made film - it eventually reached television screens a few years later under the title *Pilot Royal* - which took a not too serious look at life on this part of the course. Made in silent movie slapstick mould, complete with speeded up motion, ornamental captions and honky-tonk piano accompaniment, the film charted the trainee Prince's not too successful progress in taking revenge on his cruel and heartless instructor.

Prince Charles' trip proved arguably the most popular of his bachelorhood. It was there and then in Canada in 1975, that the word Charlie-mania was first coined. Avid young girls strove to outdo their counterparts in Australia and smothered him with kisses; in Toronto, the *Daily Star* graphically described how 'blue-rinsed matrons nearly pushed the Prince's police escorts into glass-panelled walls' in their determination to feast their eyes upon him; and even he had to admit the paramount need to maintain a decent distance from any girl he happened to speak to 'in case she gets sized up as my future spouse'. Although Prince Charles revisited Canada in every one of the following five years - including twice for the Olympic or Commonwealth Games, and twice

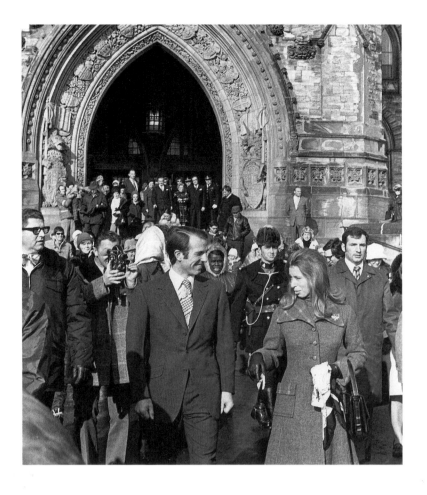

OPPOSITE PAGE, LEFT: Princess Anne and portrait at Kelowna Park, B.C. in 1971, and RIGHT: with advice from father, she cuts a centennial cake at Prince Rupert. ABOVE: Princess Anne with her husband after a visit to the House of Commons in January 1974. ABOVE RIGHT: dancing with Prime Minister Trudeau at a Government House party during the same visit, and below with Mrs Trudeau at a toboggan party there.

as President of the International Council of United World Colleges - the momentum of unquestioning popularity was never equal to what that adventurous and photogenic sojourn of 1975 achieved.

But for colour and local interest, you could not beat his Silver Jubilee Year visit, undertaken as part of an entire year of exhausting world travel, to celebrate the hundredth anniversary of the signing of the Treaty No 7, in which the Blackfoot, Blood, Peigan, Sarcee and Stony tribes of the American Red Indians ceded large tracts of the prairies to Queen Victoria. Despite the periodic reminder delivered to every member of the Royal Family that the Indians do have legitimate rights to lands long ago assumed by stealth or given away under duress or undue influence, the tribes of Alberta were on this occasion proud enough of their royal association. Prince Charles was honoured by being installed as a chieftain of their Kainai tribe, taking the title of His Royal Highness Prince Red Crow, being tricked out in full Red Indian leather and feather trappings of, appropriately enough, red, white and blue. His magnificent fluffy white headdress blew stiffly in the breeze, he was daubed with war paint and, with a Queen Elizabeth II medallion gleaming anachronistically around his neck, he cheerfully puffed at the tribal peace-pipe. Like the Earl of Athlone before him, he joined in one of the host's campfire dances, and it says a lot for his appreciation of the gesture that made him a lifelong honorary Indian that he chose a photograph of himself in this tribal regalia for his personal Christmas card that December.

His itinerary that year also took him to Calgary where, like several royal predecessors, he opened the annual Stampede. Despite his father's mild, off-the-cuff protest eight years before, he gladly accepted, and wore, a spanking new stetson, as part of a casual rig which included a wide-squared shirt and a bootlace tie. It may have been seen as an anti-climax that he appeared for the opening ceremony astride a very tame and docile horse which failed to buck once and so deprived the photographers of a chance to capture royal dignity in the act of being lost!

LAKEFIELD AND AFTER: THE BLOODING OF PRINCE ANDREW

With him on that one occasion was his younger brother Andrew, who by then had come to the end of his two-term secondment to Lakefield College near Trenton, Ontario. Lakefield College, then within two years of its centenary, was a prestigious institution of some 240 pupils whose education paralleled, at least in general terms, the sort of instruction and preparation for life which Prince Andrew was receiving at Gordonstoun.

Gordonstoun ran exchange schemes with other similar schools throughout the Commonwealth and it had long been tacitly agreed that, in view of the benefits that Prince Charles had gained from the scheme during his time at Timbertop College, near Geelong in Australia a decade earlier, both Prince Andrew and ultimately Prince Edward would be sent to schools abroad. With that sense of fair shares by which the Queen is anxious to ensure that none of her former dominions still within the Commonwealth should feel unduly hard done by, Prince Charles' stay in Australia was now counterbalanced by sending Prince Andrew to Canada, just as younger brother Edward would eventually go to New Zealand.

Prince Philip had visited Lakefield during that controversial tour of 1969, and had been sufficiently impressed by the scope it offered in all departments of personal and academic development and achievement that the decision to send his second son there was not a difficult one. For his part, the 17-year-old Prince took to his new school like a duck to water and amply justified the college's boast of good, thorough, all-round education.

Mens Sana in Copore Sano, ran its motto. The 'healthy body' found stimulation in mind' was nurtured by what the headmaster described as the 'powers of nature to educate and the encouragement of intellectual pursuits'. The 'healthy body' found stimulation in a whole range of physical opportunities, from cross-country skiing to rock-climbing, from kayaking to sailing, from seamanship to life guard patrols. Prince Andrew needed little prodding. Always a doer rather than a spectator, and eager enough to try anything once, he joined the College's hockey team, in which he was 'suitably vicious when necessary', continued with a pottery course he had started at Gordonstoun, proved himself 'really first class' on skis, joined a wind-surfing group and did some white-water paddling on the Petawa River. Of these, the hockey experiment proved the least satisfying, since he failed to qualify for the college squad, but he did prove a determined character on the boards, playing parts in anything from Bernard Shaw to *Oliver!* and laying himself open to the local theatre critics. His room-mate for most of his time at college was Donald Grant, a student some 18 months his senior, who while spending a couple of terms at Gordonstoun two years before had become a firm friend. Few privileges were accorded to the Prince, especially at communal meal times, when Andrew took his own turn at waiting on his colleagues.

Personable and good-looking, young, athletic and easy-going, Prince Andrew became the idol of Canada's young female population. His reputation as a latter day heart-throb preceded his arrival at Toronto in January, and with no little sense of embarrassment he found himself the centre of an hysterical reception from Toronto's teenage girls. They

followed him everywhere, and stories of many alleged escapades were not slow in circulating. He went skiing with Martha Anderson, a girl from Lakefield High School, and for the price of a newspaper you could read next day that she was as good as engaged to him. He then confused the issue by arranging a reunion with Sandi Jones, his much-envied escort during his previous visits to the Montreal Olympics, and when he took her sailing, then to a reception, then to a jazz concert in Toronto, local and national reporters thought they had the answer to who would be the next Duchess of York. Prince Andrew even invited her as his partner to a Lakefield College dance, then angered all the other girls there by dancing almost exclusively with her. Oblivious of their understandable envy, he gave Sandi his college scarf and badge to remember him by.

The recounting of these little incidents and gestures merely added fuel to the fires of popular passions. Hordes of young, moon-struck girls hopped along the boundaries of cricket and rugby pitches, screaming for the sporting Prince in his natty flannels or trim shorts, and half swooned every time he flashed his 'toothy smile' at them. They tried to follow him to the Orangeville Farm, 80 miles from Toronto, where he spent a weekend with friends and learned not just how to avoid admirers but also how to tap maple trees. And when on one occasion he went to Pittsburgh as one of the hundreds of supporters of his College hockey team, the attention loaded on him by the local girls there made Prince Andrew the immediate arch-enemy of their boyfriends.

There was only one sour note, and that came right at the beginning of his stay, after the Prince had given his first press conference. A local newspaper columnist turned immediately cynical and gave him a nasty dose of forthright criticism, describing him as 'this young prince in expensive blue suits, sipping ginger ale and claiming he'd like to be an ordinary

OPPOSITE PAGE, LEFT: Prince Charles arm in arm with the Northwest Territory Commissioner at Grise Fiord in 1975, and RIGHT with Pierre Trudeau after a tour of Ottawa's Parliament Buildings. TOP: three royal brothers at Montreal in 1976 to see sister Anne BELOW compete in the Olympics. ABOVE: the Queen, Prince Philip and Prince Andrew with Quebec's Premier Bourassa and Lieutenant-Governor Lapointe at a reception on board *Britannia*. BELOW: Princess Anne and Captain Phillips at a pre-Olympics press conference at Bromont.

LEFT: Prince Andrew on the ski-slopes of Cedar Mountain, near his school at Lakefield, January 1977. ABOVE: with colleagues during training for a two-week canoe expedition that summer. BELOW LEFT: as Mr Brownlow in the musical *Oliver!* which Lakefield presented in May. OPPOSITE PAGE, LEFT: Prince Charles joins Indian leaders in smoking a pipe of peace during the 1877 Treaty 7 centennial at Blackfoot Crossing in southern Alberta, and RIGHT is installed as Chief Red Crow at Calgary.

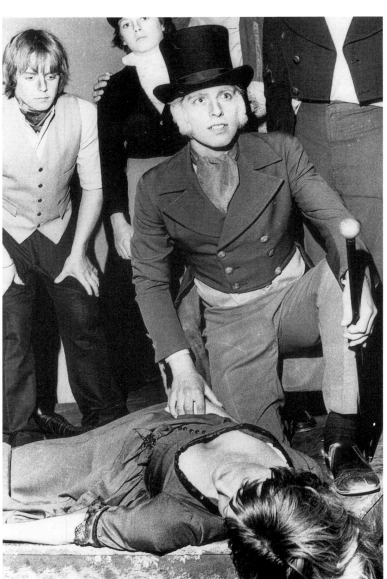

schoolboy. I do hope he brought his woollies,' it continued, in a jibe intended as a reference to a humorous complaint he had made about the cold weather, but before his six-month visit was through he proved he was equal to anything the Canadian climate could throw at him. When he linked up with Prince Charles in Calgary, he was in the middle of a whistle-stop tour which took him from the Pacific coast to regions of the Arctic Circle. Here he stopped at Resolute Bay on Cornwallis Island, as Prince Charles had two years before, and went on to Grise Fjord, where the Eskimos showed him how to build a kayak and prepare a polar bear skin for tanning. On that brief expedition he became the most northerly travelled member of the Royal Family and there is a plaqued cairn at Cape Columbia to prove it. Prince Andrew's travels also took him to Yellowknife - the world-famous gold mining centre frequently visited by his family - to three major wildlife parks, after he joined WWF Canada, and to Vancouver. Here he celebrated Canada Day and was proclaimed Soya Hun (Heir of the Earth) by the Algonquin Indians. He went sailing with the Vancouver Yacht Club and fished for salmon in the Juan de Fuca Strait, south of Victoria, where he hooked and then lost his first salmon and won the chance to go home and romance about the one that got away. He did eventually save the day by landing a three-pounder.

The vast and sometimes hostile Northwest Territories seem to possess a remarkable capacity for fascinating the Royal Family, and there was no exception in the case of Prince Andrew. Apart from a fairly brief return to Canada in 1978 the Prince was effectively prevented from visiting the country again by the demands of his naval career which began the following year. But when in 1983 he did come back it was in the Northwest Territories that he spent the whole of his stay. It was a totally private visit, so private indeed that no one seemed to know about it until it was over. The former

headmaster at Lakefield, Terry Guest, had arranged a great outdoor expedition along the Nahanni River in the Mackenzie Mountains, and had invited Prince Andrew to join the 200 college students, former students and members of staff for the whole of the three weeks. Among them was his old room-mate Donald Grant, now 24, with whom he shared a tent, and who noticed that the Prince's recent experience in the Falkland Islands conflict had 'obviously deeply affected him. I think it has made him more aware of man's vulnerability'.

He certainly embraced all the expedition's challenges with both arms. It involved a 200-mile trip by canoe, along fast flowing waters, shooting rapids and negotiating dangerous waterfalls, and paddling through canyons hundreds of yards deep - almost a mile deep in the case of Hell's Gate. At either end of the river journey there were miles of backpacking to be slogged over some of the roughest terrain in the Canadian wilderness, and he cheerfully stalked through the wild bear country of the Broken Skull Mountain Range in a pair of green combat trousers, old shirts, black army boots and a shapeless bottle-green camouflage hat. Not all the mountains were circumvented: one day he and his team climbed up Mount Sunblood, looked down to see it loom over a 300-feet waterfall thousands of feet below, then came down again - all in torrential rain. Indeed the rain proved a persistent nuisance. At one point it didn't stop for three days, but it only drew the Prince's good humour. 'I shall have to speak to mother about fixing that,' he said. They all slept rough throughout the entire journey, for most of which they were rarely less than 200 miles from the nearest road. And when at last he returned to civilisation, it was, as one observer rather romantically put it, 'with a steely glint to his eye and a determined set to his jaw'.

Assuming, of course, that you could see his jaw. In fact he had again followed his elder brother's example by letting his beard grow, and accordingly was next seen in public with a respectable covering of bristles which gave him a rugged, weathered and healthy appearance. That produced wolf-whistles when he visited the Prince of Wales Museum at Yellowknife and it no doubt impressed the folks back at Balmoral, to whom he showed it proudly before reporting back to his naval air squadron. Beard or no beard, however, Andrew was in no doubt as to the value of the trip. One of his colleagues had said that 'he desperately wanted a chance to let his hair down in private and to meet a very personal physical challenge'. It had worked; the Prince's enthusiasm was

boundless: 'It was one of the most magnificent things I've done in my whole life,' he said, rather prematurely, considering that he was then only 22 years of age.

As Prince Edward entered into adolescence, he too was to sample the unique experience which Canada has freely offered to her Royal Family. In 1978 he joined Prince Andrew and their parents for part of that year's tour which incorporated a visit to the 11th Commonwealth Games in Edmonton. The young Prince - only a 14-year-old then - was taken on an enjoyable camping trip which introduced him to the delights of the Skyline Trail in the Rockies. Then, with Prince Philip, he inspected a potash mine - his head duly, if spectacularly, protected by what appeared to be a gold plated hard hat.

This low-key, rather experimental visit was not followed up for another nine years, when Prince Edward undertook his first solo journey to Canada. This, too, was arranged without the promise of great ceremony, almost as if the Prince's comparatively modest nature and rather studied seriousness made it inappropriate to put on lavish displays and the sort of occasions which fill the front pages of newspapers. Indeed, much of Prince Edward's time was spent in the Maritime Provinces attending to his duties as an international trustee of the Duke of Edinburgh's Award Scheme - a programme which does not normally lend itself to headline-grabbing behaviour on the part of either hosts or guest.

THE OLYMPIC PRINCESS: LOOKING TOWARDS 2032

Back in 1976, Canada achieved something of a 'first' among all Commonwealth nations by hosting not just the Queen and Prince Philip, but all four of their children too, simultaneously - the only occasion when all six have been together outside Britain. That was a generally happy tour, coming as it did hard on the heels of a hectic visit to America's east coast in celebration of her independence bicentennial, and embracing the formality of official duties and the homely joys of watching horses and riders at work in that year's Olympics, which the Queen had opened before 70,000 people in Montreal. It began with a stately arrival on board the Royal Yacht *Britannia* at Halifax, and included an early visit to Fredericton, New Brunswick, where the Queen received from the representatives of the Micmac and Maliseet tribes of Indians loyal addresses petitioning for redress of their grievances against what they saw as the disregard of George III's guarantees of 1763 for their land and community rights. This pointed, though civilised, incident and the still simmering Quebec issue prompted the Queen to make coexistence the theme of her speeches throughout her tour, with the emphasis on how the concept of one nation can prevail despite the multiplicity of languages and cultural traditions.

Eventually, *Britannia* reached Kingston, Ontario, where the Queen invited the Trudeaus on board to watch the final heats of the Olympic sailing events. Margaret Trudeau felt decidedly let down by the absence of ostentatious luxury on the royal yacht and dismayed by the 'overstuffed, faded chintz sofas; bland, wishy-washy colours; and total lack of elegance.' But there were social and state occasions to compensate for Mrs Trudeau's disappointed expectations. At a dinner for 300 in Ottawa, she decided to compromise Prince Charles, and arranged for herself to sit next to him, having chosen to wear a dress with a daringly plunging neckline. Eventually, she invited him onto the dance floor. 'I knew I'd got him interested,' she reported later. 'He deliberately peeked down my blouse.' She caught him doing so, and he duly blushed, explaining in his apologetic embarrassment that 'my father always told me to look into my partner's eyes when she is wearing a low-cut dress'. 'Feast ye while ye may,' retorted the temptress: 'if I wasn't three months pregnant, there would be nothing to see!'

The Royal Family joined ranks at Bromont, where Princess Anne was competing in the Olympic equestrian event. Prince Charles had actually passed up the opportunity to play in a couple of international polo matches in England in order to be in Canada that week, justifying his temporary abandonment of his favourite sport on the grounds that Princess Anne had

up to then been doing very well, and 'it's not every day that you can watch your sister with a chance of winning an Olympic gold.'

Princess Anne had never been quite so optimistic. Some months earlier she had been mildly surprised even to find herself on the Olympic shortlist. 'If I get to Montreal, I will consider that to be an achievement,' she said at the time, 'and if I actually get a ride that will be quite something.' But go to Montreal she did, in the sharp scarlet and white outfit that became the English team uniform that summer and, upon her own insistence, without the special privileges of royalty while she was quartered with her fellow competitors in the heavily guarded Olympic village. She was, characteristically for a person of her demanding standards, impressed by the excellent training facilities and by the lush riverside pastures and thickly wooded hills of Bromont - 'much greener than in England, and the horses appreciate that,' she enthused.

Unhappily it was not to be Princess Anne's year. Her horse Goodwill proved over-excitable; suffused with vitality, he made several mistakes in the dressage. The Princess herself, acutely attuned to the importance of the occasion, found that she was perhaps too sensitive to its hushed audience. There seemed, following the announcer's special plea for quiet, to be an electric silence as she rode Goodwill out: 'I could hear things that I would never usually hear,' she commented afterwards. Worst of all, she was by no means at home in the boggy conditions which followed some heavy downpours of rain, while the steep gradients and testing fence layout of a twisting endurance course proved too much for her. At the nineteenth fence, Goodwill slipped on a patch of soft, wet sand and mud, and horse and rider went down together. Princess Anne was temporarily concussed, though not nearly as seriously as during a three-day event in Dorset four months earlier, and she eventually retired. Later she changed her mind, completed the course, and emerged from the competition with 24th place and an enhanced reputation for sheer pluck to show for it.

Her husband, Captain Mark Phillips, accompanied her to Montreal that year, though only as a reserve in the English equestrian team. He did not compete in the Games, though he was to return to Canada in 1977 and 1978 to ride for the British team in the Nations Cup at Calgary. He wasn't entirely inactive at the 1976 Olympics, however. True to his reputation as a practical joker he decided to plan an assault upon the Olympic flagstaffs, filching a flag to take home being regarded as the ultimate achievement off the course. So, one evening, and with the assistance of some of his security men,

he shinned up one of the many flagpoles, unhitched a flag - and then noticed the approach of the police. Captain Phillips and his confederates dashed back into their car, gave the police the slip, hid the flag in some bushes, and came back a day later to retrieve it when the hue and cry was safely over. Eventually, the flag returned to England with him, and if you know in which of Gatcombe Park's lavatories to look, the evidence of the ill-gotten gain will still be there.

Both Princess Anne and her husband paid brief visits to Canada together in the twelve months following their wedding in November 1973. During an extended honeymoon, they travelled to Ottawa in January 1974 to meet the Queen who was on her way to Australia to open that country's Parliament. The young couple took the opportunity to visit Ottawa's own Parliament building and the National Arts Centre and, following a century-long royal tradition, joined in a skating session on the Rideau Canal, where they mingled happily and informally with members of the public. They were also invited to a skating and tobogganing party with Governor-General Léger and Prime Minister Trudeau at Rideau Hall, and watched a hockey match at Hull.

A slightly longer visit ten months later took them to the 1974 Royal Agricultural Winter Fair at Toronto as guests of Mr John McDougald, the exhibition's past president. Not surprisingly, they were especially interested in the showjumping competition which formed part of the Winter Fair programme, though the proceedings were momentarily interrupted when a man tried to climb into the royal box to hand Princess Anne a religious pamphlet. The Princess, who only a few months before, had been the victim of an attempted kidnapping in London, did not seem half so shaken by this incident as later by the sight of a life-size model of herself which had been cleverly sculpted in butter. 'What a horror!' she gasped. For the remainder of their stay in Toronto, equestrian pursuits dominated. The royal couple visited Toronto Races and the Prix des Nations equestrian event, and went riding at Norcliffe Farm with the chairman of Ontario Jockey Club - the Princess, appropriately, astride a

OPPOSITE PAGE, LEFT: the Queen, Prince Philip and Prince Andrew, in Edmonton for the Commonwealth Games, waving to crowds from the balcony of Government House in August 1978. RIGHT: Princes Edward and Andrew line up in the cafeteria of the Athletes' Village for lunch. ABOVE: Princess Anne, during her visit to Toronto in November 1979, inspecting a replica of a Canadian beaver presented to her while she was attending *Kick for Cansave*, an event organised by the Canadian Save the Children Fund, at City Hall. RIGHT: Prince Charles guides a rescue boat from Pearson College during a 1979 tour of the institution. College director Jack Matthew holds on behind.

horse called Royalty.

The Princess came back to Canada again - and alone - in October 1979, visiting Save the Children Fund centres in Ottawa and Ontario. Three years later, following a lengthy and sometimes controversial trip to the USA, she spent a further twelve days in what by then was a fully independent country, carrying out a programme of more general public and private engagements. Her schedule in Ottawa included the opening of an entrance for the disabled at Government House - one of the results of the Year of the Disabled over which her uncle, Lord Snowdon, had presided the previous year - and a boat-trip down the Rideau Canal. These were fairly staid duties compared with her two days in the Yukon amid speculation that the region would become Canada's eleventh province before long. Here, she experienced that breathtaking aspect of Canada with which her brother and father were so familiar. She was taken on an exciting helicopter tour of the Elias Mountains and Kluane Glacier; she rode in a paddle-wheeler down the Yukon River, went down a copper mine at Whitehorse, and visited an Indian co-operative. The glories of nature in all her unpredictable fury even followed her to an official banquet where she ate to the sometimes terrifying sounds of a freak thunderstorm.

Princess Anne moved on to Saskatoon and Regina, to which she had been invited to celebrate the centenaries of the two cities. In the course of the visit to Saskatoon, she was asked to pencil in another engagement in her diary - for a return journey in the year 2032. Without a doubt, the Princess Royal, if she lives to be 82, will be there to reclaim a time capsule which she had on the 1982 visit just closed up, and re-open it to celebrate the city's sesquicentenary. If she does, she will have emulated her grandmother, who herself visited Canada in her 82nd year. It was in Saskatchewan, too, that Princess Anne learned that the Regina Rifle Regiment - once mocked as the Farmer John's - had been given the prefix 'Royal', and that the Queen had appointed her as its Colonel-in-Chief. It was the sort of timing that thrilled the citizens of Regina, as indeed Princess Anne's visit to Gravelburg in the south of the province thrilled the Mayor of this mainly French-speaking town. He assured her that although 'only a few in our community have their roots in Great Britain, there is a strong and faithful loyalty to the Crown.'

By the time her tour of Saskatchewan was over, the Princess had spent longer in the province than any of her royal relations ever. She treated the record with a mixture of pride and modesty: 'It's rare to be one up on the rest of the family,' she admitted. The remainder of her Canadian visit that year was spent in Manitoba, where she crossed the Red River near Selkirk in remembrance of La Vérendrye's expeditions and settlement, and attended a casual, country-style party at Brandon. And it is a nice reflection of her appreciation towards her Canadian hosts that, during the course of the tour, the Princess made her own personal contribution to the equestrian life of Canada by promising to send over a foal by her Persian stallion, which she hoped might be crossed with a small North American pony to create a new Canadian breed. That was probably the most original, and practical, royal gesture of all.

OPPOSITE PAGE: Prince Charles was back in Victoria in 1980 to meet more students of Pearson College. ABOVE: a hard-hatted and headlamped Princess Anne, holding a bouquet of fireweed, tours the Whitehorse Copper Mine 700 feet down. ABOVE RIGHT: Prince Charles at Pearson College, Victoria, again in 1982: this wharf began to sink under the weight of the hundred or so people who joined him on it! BELOW LEFT: Princess Anne at McCain Foods, Grand Falls, N.B. in June 1986, and below watching the British bobsleigh team in Calgary training for the 1988 winter Olympics.

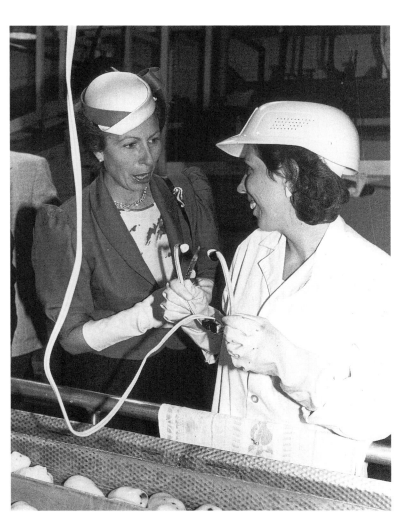

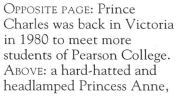

CHAPTER FIVE

SISTERS, COUSINS AND AUNTS

It is tempting to confine the concept of royal visits - whether to Canada or anywhere else - to those involving the sovereign and immediate members of the sovereign's family. Understandable though this may be, particularly in the telescopic light of history, it should not be forgotten that, in the last thirty-five years, many less senior ranked members of the Royal Family have contributed to Canada's enviable status as the country most frequently and fully visited by royalty. The Kent family, for instance, accounts for almost a dozen visits, including the more memorable ones such as that in 1954, when Princess Marina brought her popular seventeen-year-old daughter, Princess Alexandra over; the 1968 visit of the Duke and Duchess of Kent to the Calgary Stampede; and the rather more unusual visit of Prince Michael to Cape Breton Island to preside over the official celebrations of yet another birthday: the 75th anniversary of the first powered flight - that of the Silver Dart in 1909 - within the Empire. Prince Michael had visited Canada alone on two previous occasions: once in 1973, when he joined the British bobsleigh team during the World Championships in Montreal; and again the following year, when he visited Ottawa with the British Ministry of Defence with whom he was then employed. Shortly after his marriage to Marie-Christine von Reibnitz, he brought her to Toronto for a brief visit, and the couple came to Montreal in 1980.

Prince Michael's sister, Princess Alexandra, first came to Canada with her mother, the then Duchess of Kent, in 1954, but it was not for another thirteen years that she set foot in the country again. Although by then she was married, with two very young children, and was not disposed to travel abroad for long periods, she did accept an invitation to tour Canada for a total of 25 days in May and June of 1967. The visit was well planned, full of variety and, it being 1967, full of reminders that this was centenary year. Indeed, the word 'Centennial' was everywhere. The Princess attended a centennial ball at Toronto's Moss Park Armouries, opened the Centennial Stadium at the University of Victoria, visited the Centennial Museum in Vancouver, watched a performance of the centennial musical *Wild Rose* in Calgary, presented centennial medallions to students at Brandon College (which became a University the same day when she handed over a royal charter), was herself presented with centennial gifts at a centennial awards dinner in Winnipeg, took lunch at tables decorated with shastri daisies and centennial roses, and of course visited *Expo 67* in Montreal.

Another centennial - that of the birth of her grandmother, Queen Mary, was recalled when the Princess opened the Queen Mary Collection of children's books at Toronto's public library; while her great-grandmother, Queen Alexandra, was commemorated at the 109-foot Alexandra Falls at Hay River in Northwest Territories and her great-great-grandmother, Queen Victoria, rated a special ceremony, *Salute to Queen Victoria*, at the city that bears her name. There was nearly another centennial show at the Royal Ontario Museum, where the Torontonians put on an exhibition trendily entitled *Modesty to Mod*; which managed to cover the history of Canadian costume for only 97, and not a hundred, years.

Princess Alexandra was accorded a range of royal transport which by now has become habitual on long tours. Most of her journeying from province to province was done by air, but her trip from Vancouver to Banff was undertaken by CPR train, leaving Vancouver an hour before midnight, and arriving at Banff at 7.30 the following evening - with a useful 36 hours of freedom to follow before the next royal engagement! At Calgary, the Princess toured Heritage Park by stage-coach and train, and at Edmonton, took one of her journeys from her hotel to Victoria Park by vintage car. Then, during her visit to Winnipeg, she was taken to Kildonan Park by paddlewheel steamship, and thence to the park's pavilion by horse-drawn brougham. And, when the tour was over, she left Canada by ship - the *Empress of Canada* - from Montreal.

The comprehensive nature of the tour also gave the Princess the chance to meet a very wide cross-section of Canadians. There was a mass of Girl Guides and Brownies in Pioneer Square to greet her as she emerged from Christ Church Cathedral during her stay in Victoria; she met leaders of ethnic communities at the Ontario Folk Art Festival in Maple Leaf Gardens, Toronto; Indian chiefs and cowboys were presented to her during the interval of the musical in Calgary; a representative selection of students from Edmonton schools attended her visit to the city's Victoria Composite High School; while at Whitehorse, her bouquet was given by a little Indian girl by the very un-Indian name of Edith Smith. At Brandon, Princess Alexandra almost got lost amongst a crowd of 7,000 children - and, it must be said, seemed thoroughly to relish the experience, though probably not as much as she enjoyed her meeting with Winnipeg's most familiar resident, 73-year-old organ-grinder Charlie Smith. He played her a couple of tunes, while his pet monkey looked

OPPOSITE: the Duchess of Kent, Princess Alexandra and Vincent Massey at The Citadel, Quebec in August 1954.

93

bemusedly on, and then presented her with a couple of pairs of nylon stockings wrapped in white tissue paper!

Princess Alexandra's husband, the Hon. Angus Ogilvy (as he then was) accompanied her on this tour, and the nature of the Princess' engagements at certain points made it appropriate that the two of them should go their separate ways. With Mr Ogilvy's many business interests - he then held over fifty directorships in the City of London and was Director of the 117 Group of Investment Trusts - some time was accordingly set aside for him to met his counterparts in Canada. Thus, in Toronto, he lunched at the Canadian Imperial Bank of Commerce (on whose Board he then sat), and visited the Minister of Industrial Development. He met local businessmen in Calgary, visited industrial areas in Edmonton, economic developments in Yellowknife, and the Canadian Wheat Board in Winnipeg. And at Brandon, he met a restaurant owner whose great-great-grandfather married the sister of Mr Ogilvy's great-great-grandmother. 'Look, dear,' he called out to the Princess. 'I've got some relations here.' But his wife didn't have the time: 'Come along before you find any more family!' she replied.

Meanwhile, on the tourist trail, the royal couple witnessed a superb Voyageur canoe pageant at Edmonton (Mr Ogilvy being the official starter for the subsequent canoe sprint), walked along Winnipeg's Memorial Boulevard, which had been the scene of recent rioting by beatniks, watched a miniature rodeo in Calgary, were treated to an exhibition of square-dancing after a Provincial dinner in Regina, toured the Planetarium at Winnipeg, and surveyed the growing mass of downtown Toronto from the observation platform of the Dominion Centre tower.

When, thirteen years later, the Princess returned to Toronto, she was given an even more comprehensive view of an even more burgeoning city when she was taken to the top of the new CN Tower. She was rivetted by the sight of the city rapidly sprawling in all directions and the lake spreading out below her, and her reactions made the Tower an obligatory stop on many future royal itineraries. There was, however, very little sightseeing for the Princess on this trip, which was largely devoted to engagements and meetings with the two regiments of which she is Colonel-in-Chief - the Queen's

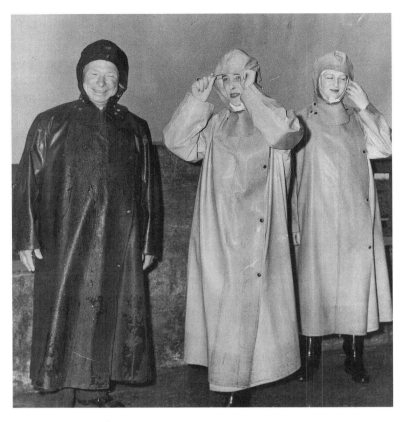

Own Rifles of Canada, then celebrating its 120th birthday, and the Canadian Scottish Regiment. Indeed, during the ten-day tour, which took the Princess to Nanaimo and Victoria as well as Toronto, she attended three regimental lunches, two dinners, four inspections, a wreath-laying ceremony and no fewer than eight receptions.

In between those two visits, Princess Alexandra returned to Toronto late in 1967 for a British Week, and paid a brief visit to Nova Scotia in 1973. Her most recent visit, in 1985, was again confined to Toronto, and again heavily weighted in favour of the Queen's Own Rifles. Indeed, it was with them that she spent the final two days of her short visit, witnessing their paratroopers rigging their equipment at CFB Borden, watching a paradrop from a Hercules aircraft, inspecting their tanks, and cutting, with a glistening ceremonial sword, a huge anniversary cake at a splendid regimental dinner at the Hilton Harbour Castle Hotel. All of which shows how, quite apart from centenaries and bicentenaries, even a 125th anniversary - as this was for the regiment - could legitimately be regarded as yet another good reason for celebrating in the presence of royalty!

A TOUCH OF HIGHLAND COURTESY:
WILLIAM OF GLOUCESTER

It is somewhat odd that, of all the branches of the Royal Family, the Gloucesters have played such a small part, officially at least, in the long saga of royal visits to Canada. Prince Henry, the first Duke, visited the country briefly in 1929, but his wife, whom he married in 1935, has never toured Canada officially in the whole of her long life. Her son, the present Duke, paid a short visit to Ottawa in 1983, to commemorate the centenary of the foundation of the Canadian Priory of the Order of St John of Jerusalem, but it is ironic that the longest - and without doubt the best enjoyed - visit was that paid by his elder brother, the late Prince William, during his university days.

Prince William was a much travelled young man, with a lively and questing nature, whose undergraduate days were

spent, not in one of the British universities, but at the Californian university of Stanford. Making the most of his opportunities, he devised, with a friend of his - Tom Troubridge, the future first husband of Princess Michael of Kent - a grand tour of central and north America, which they completed in the summer of 1964 with a visit to various Canadian cities. Being August, of course, one would not expect the weather to have been a problem, as it had been at the start of many another royal tour - and indeed, for once, it wasn't. But problems there were all the same. The Prince and his companion had arrived at Quebec City's Citadel by prior arrangement with their host, Governor-General Vanier, only to find their way barred by a French-Canadian sentry. Not only did his questions as to their identity and business put Prince William's apparently elementary French to the test, but he also refused to believe his story when he did at last manage to express it. Eventually help arrived, and the militia guarding the fort were subsequently properly briefed. So well, in fact, that on the eventual departure of the Prince and his friend, dressed less than formally in jeans and rakish berets, they were greeted by a crisp and snappy presentation of arms as they shuffled through the main gate straight into a crowd of bemused tourists.

After cursory visits to Montreal, Ottawa and Toronto, the two travellers swung south back into the States, then north towards Winnipeg and Regina. They found little to interest them in the prairie country, except the little township of Barnwell, which Prince William surmised had been named after his parents' country home in Northamptonshire. At any rate, he celebrated the discovery by having his photograph

OPPOSITE PAGE, TOP: the
Queen Mother receiving
guests at the Columbia
University Charter Day
dinner in New York, on her
way to the first tour of

Canada of her widowhood.
BOTTOM: dwarfed by the
National War Memorial in
Ottawa, during Armistice
week, 1954. ABOVE: seated
beneath portraits of King

George V and Queen Mary
at a State dinner given by
Govenor-General
Massey at Government
House, Ottawa. BELOW LEFT:
meeting the Black Watch

pipers who led the guests in.
BELOW RIGHT: the Queen
Mother meeting veterans of
both wars in Ottawa.

LEFT: the Princess Royal receiving her law degree at Laval University, Quebec early in her 1955 tour of Canada. BELOW LEFT: with engineering students during her visit to Queen's University, and BELOW the Princess is shown a 19th-century cannon during a visit to Old Fort Henry, Ontario. BOTTOM LEFT: with officers of the Royal Canadian Corps of Signals, she watches a dispatch-rider display at Vimy Barracks, Kingston, Ontario, where BOTTOM RIGHT she later took tea in the Sergeants' Mess. OPPOSITE PAGE, TOP: visiting the stables of industrialist E.P. Taylor at Windfields Farm, near Toronto. BOTTOM: talking to a five-year-old polio victim who learned to walk again, at the Red Cross HQ in Toronto.

taken as he swung from the road sign at the entrance to the township - much to the amazement of passing motorists.

Their destination was British Columbia, where they arrived early in September, and where they began three weeks of strenuous outdoor life. With local help they established and ran their own camps, the Prince taking his turn to fell small trees in order to cut firewood. They then began their training with some long-distance hikes through forests over which loomed 'horrifying peaks and glaciers', acclimatised themselves gradually to walking at high altitudes, and progressed towards their ultimate aim of grizzly-bear shooting.

Prince William had already been surprised by a black bear at one camp when, on his way back to the cabin, he saw it casually munching its way through a packet of cookies. He gave what his friend described as 'a strangled cry' and hurtled away from it 'like a guided missile', clearing an intervening stream in a single, terrified leap. But the experience didn't lessen his enthusiasm for the expedition, and he spent a fascinating time locating and hunting grizzlies.

He was also enchanted by both the scenery and the people of the province. In a letter to his parents back in England he wrote, 'This is magnificent country; moreover, the people are absolutely delightful. It reminded me very much of Scotland and there is a lot of Highland courtesy and charm to be found.' It seems from that, that Canada could well have become the subject of greater familiarisation for the Prince, had not his premature and tragic death intervened. He was killed when his light aircraft crashed in an air race near Wolverhampton, England in 1972.

LA PRINCESSE MARY: A BREATH OF OLD-WORLD CHARM

It has often been said that it is easy for any country to stage great welcomings and programmes full of interest and spectacle if the guest is sufficiently important. Presumably the effort involved in entertaining, for instance, the present Prince and Princess of Wales is justified by the prestige which comes with the occasion and the publicity which puts any province, city, town or community on the map, if even only for a few days. It is therefore rather curious to us today to realise that less than forty years ago, cities throughout Canada were pulling out all the stops for a member of the Royal Family who was no more than tenth in line to the Throne. She was Princess Mary, the only daughter of George V, so modest and retiring a soul as to be rarely the subject of newspaper reports or pictures in her own country, or much known in others. But, in the wake of the succession of glamorous royal events that had occurred since the end of the war, the cachet of royalty, even among the lesser-known members of the British Royal Family, was sufficiently strong for them to be invited to undertake lengthy and quite comprehensive tours of Commonwealth countries and to be treated every bit as enthusiastically as a reigning sovereign. In this connection, the example of Princess Mary is a typical one.

Princess Mary, born in 1897 and created Princess Royal in 1932, had married the future 6th Earl of Harewood in 1922, and had been widowed in 1947. Of her two sons, the elder, the present Earl, had been a prisoner of war in Colditz and on his release had served as ADC to the Earl of Athlone during the latter months of his Governor-Generalship of Canada. Unlike most members of the Royal Family, the Princess Royal had never visited Canada, though like many of her royal relatives, she enjoyed the status of Colonel-in-Chief of Canadian regiments. It was in that capacity that in 1955 she came to Canada for almost a full month's tour which was as busy and varied, and in many respects as enthusiastically heralded and attended, as one would have expected for the Queen herself.

ABOVE: The Princess Royal with Lady Baden-Powell at Government House, Victoria in October 1955. BELOW LEFT: with veteran Captain Grey (and chihuahua) at Victoria's Veterans' Hospital. BELOW: supermarket shopping at Supervalu at Oak Bay Junction – a new experience for the Princess.

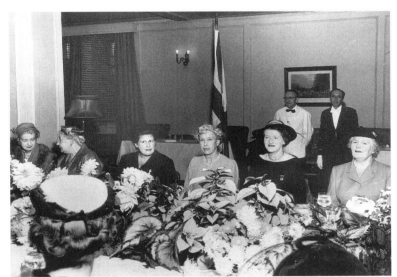

ABOVE: the royal C-in-C with her Canadian Scottish Regiment after awarding 'Wee Andy' McGeorge the Canadian Forces Decoration BOTTOM LEFT at the Royal Athletic Park, Victoria. LEFT: lunching with Victoria's IODE officers and BELOW with her suite, a signed memento for the Princess.

Princess Margaret's first and memorable visit to Canada in 1958. LEFT: with Lieutenant-Governor Ross *en route* for City Hall, Toronto. BELOW: bad weather but good spirits at Camp Gagetown, N.B. BOTTOM: inspecting the Royal Canadian Engineers outside Victoria's Legislature. OPPOSITE PAGE, TOP LEFT: the Princess being greeted by Indian Chiefs at Nanaimo, B.C., where she made the first cut TOP RIGHT into a 10,000-lb centennial cake. BOTTOM: just in time, the red carpet is rolled out for Princess Margaret at Penticton, B.C.

She arrived, as was the leisurely custom of those days, by ship - the *Empress of France* - with other passengers, many of whom were on their way to set up home in Canada. On the journey, she had seen her first whale in the Gulf of St Lawrence and, like any other passenger, had had her passport stamped before disembarking. Bad weather delayed her arrival at Quebec by a day, and the bunting that had done good service in 1939 was soon soaked as it was brought out again for this occasion. Within a few hours, she was being accorded the full royal treatment with a State banquet at the Citadel, for which she wore a tiara which once belonged to Queen Victoria, and the robe that she herself had worn at Elizabeth II's coronation. There was further special preference for the Princess at Montreal's McGill University, where the doctorate awarded successively to the future Edward VII in 1860, the future George V in 1901, the future Edward VIII in 1919 and the future Elizabeth II in 1951 was now, on Founders' Day, conferred upon this somewhat withdrawn royal personality. According to the citation, the degree was awarded for her 'splendid example during the dark days of World War I and encouragement in the years that followed. She has enhanced the care of the sick and fostered the welfare of children.' These were rather ponderous and heavily worded references to her V.A.D. work in the First World War, and her patronage of the Girl Guide movement and the Women's Royal Army Corps, but she nevertheless accepted the award with due graciousness and added it to the four similar honorary degrees she had already received from various British universities. By that time - less than a week after her arrival - she was able to say that she felt 'quite at home in the beautiful province of Quebec, about which I have heard so much from my family who have been here before me.'

Her regimental duties were dispatched in predictable manner: at Kingston, Ontario, her day with the Royal Corps of Signals at Vimy Barracks included the usual inspections and ceremonies, as well as the more unusual experience of stepping into an ice-box for a couple of minutes to get a taste of simulated climatic conditions. Later in the tour, she spent another day with her other regiment, the Canadian Scottish Regiment (Princess Mary's), and admitted to them that she was so delighted to see them all for the first time in full dress

uniform. There were other service connections, such as her visit to Deer Lodge Military Hospital in Winnipeg, where she took a hurried coffee break with a group of Old Contemptibles; her introduction to some World War I veterans who talked about the brass tobacco boxes they had received from her in 1914; and her meeting with members of the British Naval Officers Association of British Columbia at the Trafalgar Day Ball in Vancouver.

Among the less formal interludes, the view over Ottawa from the Peace Tower offered her what she later described as 'a breathtaking sight', while at a tea-party given at the Lieutenant-Governor 's suite at Toronto, she noticed, with the perception which seems to bless most members of the Royal Family, that the carpet was the same blue and gold colour and of the same design as one at Marlborough House when her mother, Queen Mary, had lived there. At Niagara, she saw the Falls only through a heavy downpour of rain, which had in any event delayed her visit there by half an hour; and when she was told of the Hill family's attempt to shoot the rapids in a barrel, she refused to admire the venture. Instead, she simply said, 'Oh, what a stupid thing to do!' She herself showed rather more prudence when she resisted the temptation to touch some poison ivy which she had asked to see during a visit to the Botanical Gardens in Montreal. At Victoria, she became the first member of the Royal Family to shop at a supermarket, when she visited the Super-Valu store near Oak Bay Junction. She was impressed by its electronic eye door, and bought a few articles, especially from the frozen food counter, before waiting in line to pay at the check-out. Supermarkets had not yet been introduced into Britain, and the Princess had expressly requested to visit one in Canada, though only on condition that the event was not publicised in advance. Accordingly, the other shoppers in the store were as annoyed to realise what they had missed as the manager was relieved that he had had the place cleaned out beforehand!

Of all the people she met, perhaps the least surprising was a Dionne quin: on this occasion, Marie was the choice for a

ABOVE: Princess Margaret riding in a stagecoach to a rodeo at Williams Lake, B.C., and BELOW LEFT passing cattle pens there. Earlier she had met an eighteen-year-old Indian princess OPPOSITE PAGE, TOP in the town. BELOW: a watchful Sergeant-at-Arms precedes HRH to Vancouver's City Hall. OPPOSITE PAGE, BOTTOM LEFT: the royal motorcade at Banff. BOTTOM RIGHT: at a reception at the Château Laurier Hotel, Ottawa with Prime Minister Diefenbaker.

royal meeting, having recently joined the Convent of La Congrégation des Servants du Très Saint Laurent in Quebec as a novitiate. At Montreal General Hospital, she tried a few words of Inuit to a 19-year-old appendicitis patient during a visit at which she was amused to learn that a bumper crop of girls had been born there that day - one of which was named Mary in her honour. There were more personal meetings, too, such as that at Fort Henry, Ontario, where the Princess met a tailor, John Spencer, who had served with her husband during World War I; at Montreal, where an architect, Peter Baroff, was discovered to have been interned as a prisoner of war with the Princess' son; and at E.P. Taylor's stud at Windfields Farm, where she was surprised to find a groom who had formerly worked at her own Newmarket stable.

One or two of her more formal contacts were equally memorable: Mayor Witton of Ottawa distinguished herself by arriving late for the farewell ceremonies at the station, then running along the platform as the Princess' train pulled out, in a desperate, and in events vain, attempt to shake her hand. Mayor Drapeau of Montreal made an even more unfortunate gaffe when, having seen the Princess to her car after a reception at City Hall, he immediately turned to go inside again, leaving the Princess waving to his back as the car drove off. But he redeemed himself later: at a dinner in a chalet on St Helen's Island on the St Lawrence, the royal visitor stubbed her toe on a cable and stumbled, and it was Mayor Drapeau who came to the rescue to prevent her from falling to the ground.

The 24-day tour took the Princess Royal to eight provincial capitals and major cities and, despite its smooth running, was enough to test the stamina of most 58-year-olds. On her first full day in Montreal, for instance, she had no fewer than 21 engagements, during one of which she shook hands with 452 people. In Ottawa she was, somewhat patronisingly perhaps, commended for the 'brisk, no-nonsense movements' with which she shovelled earth around the roots of the tree she was planting at Government House, while at Toronto, she

OPPOSITE PAGE: the Queen Mother presents centenary colours to the Black Watch at Montreal, 1962. ABOVE LEFT: with Quebec's Premier Lesage at a Provincial luncheon in Montreal. ABOVE: the Queen Mother with an ox-team driver at an Ontario exhibition of 19th-century farming life, Morrisburg.

regretted that her busy schedule left her no time to sample a ride on the city's subway. In addition to the restrictions of that tight programme, she had to contend with the prevailing speculation about the future of Princess Margaret, whose romance with Group Captain Peter Townsend was headline news every day. No wonder that at Toronto, the Lieutenant Governor made a point of relating how the Princess Royal had discussed hunting and fishing with him. 'I imagine,' he suggested, ' that she wouldn't mind a bit of hunting and fishing instead of all the rounds.'

Typically, she had asked for no frills or fuss. Equally typically, Canada gave her both. Squads of siren-wailing motorcades escorted her around Montreal; at Kingston, the Royal Corps of Signals gave her a $3,000 mink stole; Ottawa's reception for her was, despite the frequency of royal visits to the capital, heartwarming to say the least, and a reception at Rideau Hall at which she was guest-of-honour was described as 'all brocades and tiaras, the most brilliant event of the social season.' In Toronto, Mayor Phillips said that there was no happier occasion than when Toronto entertained a member of the Royal Family, while at Victoria, it took the screaming engines of the Princess' aircraft to drown out the cheers of a huge crowd who had come to see her land at Patricia Bay airport. And when, eventually, she took her leave of Canada on the Empress of France from Montreal, the band played her away with a brass rendition of *So Long, It's Been Good To Know You*.

For all the welcome and hospitality of that visit, the Princess Royal might well have considered that she, a conservative, minor royal nearing her sixties, could have

TOP LEFT: the Princess Royal inspects the guard of honour at Malton Airport near Toronto to begin her second and last visit to Canada in 1962. TOP RIGHT: with Girl Guides and their officers in the grounds of the University of British Columbia. ABOVE RIGHT: the Princess inspecting soldiers of the Canadian Scottish Regiment. LEFT: signing the guest book after a tea party ABOVE with officers of the Royal Canadian Corps of Signals. OPPOSITE: the Queen Mother's 1965 visit to Canada. TOP: uniformed Red Cross ladies and nursing staff line up for her visit to the Red Cross Society Lodge at Sunny Brook Hospital, where the six-month-old baby of Mrs Laurie Morton had its toes tickled by the royal fingers. BOTTOM PICTURE: the Queen Mother sizing up the Queen's Plate runners at the Woodbine Racetrack.

little relevance to the outward-looking wide-ranging attitudes of a confident country like Canada. Canada thought otherwise, however, because seven years later, she was invited back to British Columbia, Ontario and Quebec. This time, she arrived by plane, though she had caught a cold by the time the 15-hour flight was over, and disembarked at Patricia Bay airport to the thunder of a 21-gun salute echoing across the Saanich Peninsula. 'Our royal guest will be assured of a warm reception befitting a senior member of the House of Windsor,' promised one Victoria newspaper and, sure enough, more than 8,000 people came to Beacon Hill Park to watch from the gorse-covered hill as she presented new colours to the 1st Battalion of her Canadian Scottish Regiment. Scores of people tried to occupy seats left empty by accredited photographers, and stewards had to clear them out several times. A total of 2,500 Girl Guides and Brownies assembled on the lawns of Government House, gave her the Grand Howl and broke into song for her. As this year was Victoria's centenary year, the Princess also opened the centennial Flower Show at the Curling Rink, and talked to local gardeners, one of whom had worked on the estate next to her home, Harewood House, and had been a great friend of her head ground-keeper. The city also took the opportunity to ask her to open its new courthouse, for which she was rewarded by an entertaining speech by the Attorney-General who reflected on 'the carefree days when there were no lawyers in Victoria!'

After a two-day rest in Vancouver, during which the only untoward incident was a baggage mix-up in which her equerry walked off with a police officer's suitcase, the Princess Royal flew to Kingston, Ontario. The weather here was unspeakable (suitably announced by an electric thunderstorm on her arrival) but there was work to be done and only two days to do it in. She revisited Vimy Barracks, and turned the first turf prior to the building of the gates to a Royal Corps of Signals memorial site. At the town's community centre, she tapped her feet to the rhythm of *Red River Valley* as Girl Guides and Brownies entertained her with dancing and singing. She visited several hospitals, and lunched at the Salvation Army Citadel, before driving through Kingston. One householder, a Miss Somerville, had gone to the trouble of decorating her house with no fewer that fifteen Union Jacks, on the grounds that 'I thought somebody should do something for her.'

Moving on to Toronto, she celebrated another centenary - that of the Royal Regiment of Canada - by presenting new colours in a ceremony which took place in a temperature of 85 degrees. She was coolly dressed in a white summer regimental uniform that she had helped to design, but her soldiers were not quite so lucky: over thirty of them, out of a total complement of 450, fainted in the heat. Nor was Her Royal Highness quite so lucky the following day, when a sudden shower of rain soaked her WRAC blue dress uniform as she emerged from St James's Anglican Cathedral after a service to dedicate the old colours. That evening, she attending a regimental dinner at which she told her hosts, 'For a hundred years you have served the cause of Their Majesties my great-grandmother, my grandfather, my father, my brothers and today Her Majesty the Queen - a truly royal record.' And just before her Toronto visit came to an end, the Princess attended a regimental ball at which she watched with more than a little amusement as officers and their partners tackled the Twist. She took the floor herself, though in more modest fashion, with the Canadian Army Chief of Staff, and enjoyed herself so much that she stayed for almost one and a half hours after she was due to leave.

The Princess' visit also coincided with the sixth birthday of the Park Plaza Hotel, so it was fitting that it should provide her home base for the duration. A top floor suite was taken, consisting of twelve large, airy rooms overlooking a be-spired Toronto in full summer leaf, and tactfully containing Anglo-French furniture - an English walnut dressing table here, a French armchair of carved Circassian walnut there - as well as an historic reminder of Albert Edward, Prince of Wales' 1860 visit in the shape of soup tureens and wine glasses which had been used over a century earlier. As it happened, the Princess Royal made history of her own that week, as the first woman to be installed as an honorary bencher of the 165-year-old Law Society of Upper Canada. The ceremony, at Osgoode Hall, was reminiscent of those in which her brother in 1919 and her grandfather in 1860 had also been made honorary benchers, and as the Princess was ceremonially robed in black over her floral print dress, she said simply, 'I have not been a great lawyer, but am fast becoming one.'

Her two-week tour nearly ended in embarrassment when Mayor Witton threatened to boycott the Ottawa proceedings after a blazing row in the Board of Control over parking regulations. Fortunately, though, at the last moment and without much indication that matters had been sorted out, the mayor turned up, and all smiles. After a 28-hour visit to Quebec, where she was addressed as La Princesse Mary and spoke French in return, the Princess Royal received Canada's last farewell at a State dinner at the Bois de Coulogne following a tour of the Ile d'Orléans. It was indeed a final farewell: the Princess never returned to Canada, and died quite suddenly less than three years later.

OPPOSITE PAGE: in May 1967, Princess Alexandra and her husband, the Hon Angus Ogilvy, paid their first visit to Canada together. TOP: the royal couple meet Charlie Smith, a 73-year-old organ-grinder who had been a mainstay of Winnipeg street life since the 1920s. BOTTOM LEFT: an informal moment as the Princess stops in her tracks to chat to a member of her guard of honour while her escort waits patiently. BOTTOM RIGHT: accepting a polar bear skin from Manitoba's Premier Duff Roblin at a dinner at Winnipeg's Civic Auditorium. RIGHT: the Princess and Mr Ogilvy asking a handicapped girl about a mobility aid she is using. BELOW: a royal farewell at Redwood Dock, Winnipeg from the York boat *Chappawa II*.

SHOOTING STAR: PRINCESS MARGARET MAKES HER MARK

In direct contrast to the rather staid image of the late Princess Royal came, for the first time in 1958, the Queen's younger sister, Princess Margaret. At this time Princess Margaret - a highly fashion-conscious leader of her own social 'set', still, at almost 28, the most eligible of unmarried daughters, and the subject of endless speculation as to the identity of her future husband - was a world celebrity, and the Canadians gave her a welcome of such proportions that she is unlikely ever to forget the experience.

That July, in addition to visiting Ontario, she crossed Canada to attend the centenary celebrations of British Columbia, and every town she visited feted her almost as if she were the Queen herself. Victoria's public, and many privately-owned, buildings were studded with lights; illuminated messages of welcome were strung across the streets, and the Princess received the unique anvil salute at the New Westminster City Hall. The custom, she was told, dates back to the 1870s, when the city's cannons were considered unsafe for firing, and anvils were used as depositories for the powder used in the salute. The salute is still performed annually on 24th May, in honour of Queen Victoria's birthday, but Princess Margaret's first visit to the country was deemed a worthy occasion on which to arrange an additional ceremony. It was a measure of the indulgence in which Canada then held the Princess that, of all the public compliments paid to her during that visit, that of Mayor Phillips of Toronto, who suggested that she should make Toronto her second home because its citizens regarded her as a fairy-tale princess, was perhaps the most memorable.

None of her subsequent visits ever attained that level of popularity and celebration. Like other members of her family, she, and Lord Snowdon, visited again to tour *Expo 67* in Montreal, while on their next visit - in September 1971 - the Princess officially opened Winnipeg's Art Gallery. Almost three years later, the couple returned to Winnipeg as guests of the Lieutenant-Governor of Manitoba, to join in Winnipeg's centenary festivities. Sadly, their programme constituted almost the last of their public appearances together: their lives were already drifting their separate ways, and within two years they had agreed to live apart.

Two years after her eventual divorce from Lord Snowdon in 1978, the Princess arrived in Canada alone, and for more birthday celebrations. This time, Saskatchewan and Alberta played host, for 1980 saw the 75th anniversary of their entry into the Confederation. Appropriately, at an anniversary dinner in Saskatoon, she heartily recommended the concept of 'this great Confederation which is Canada, with your Queen safely at its head.' For the rest, the well-varied royal round included visits to art galleries and museums in Saskatoon, a tour of an Indian reserve at Prince Albert and time spent with French communities at Zenon Park. By contrast, Alberta celebrated both the confederation anniversary and the royal visit with its own special panache, inviting the Princess to join in the annual Klondike Days festival at Edmonton. Though this is now a regular venue for royal ladies, this occasion was the first on which a member of the Royal Family had taken an active part in the proceedings. Princess Margaret did so in style, wearing a close-fitting Victorian dance-hall

OPPOSITE PAGE, TOP PICTURES: Princess Margaret and her husband, Lord Snowdon, visit *Expo 67* in Montreal. BOTTOM: hats off for a royal smile as Dalhousie University, N.S. awards the Queen Mother an honorary law doctorate in July 1967. BELOW LEFT: the Queen Mother inspects trainees from Cornwallis naval base on arriving in Halifax the same day. BELOW: a rare visit by the Duke and Duchess of Kent, here seen taking part in the Calgary Stampede parade in July 1968.

costume in raw silk and an opulently feathered hat for a celebration barbecue laid on in her honour.

It was unfortunate, to say the least, that this particular royal visit (and there have been similar examples since) was marred by a scathing personal attack upon the Princess. Hard on the heels of a torrent of adverse publicity surrounding her friendship with Roddy Llewellyn, the press found a genuine welcome difficult to offer, though few newspapers went as far as the Toronto *Sun*, which uncompromisingly referred to her, simply and damningly, as 'a royal baggage'. But worse was to follow the next year when, in the wake of some disturbing developments in Northern Ireland, which included the deaths of ten internees on hunger strike, the Princess became the butt, during her five-day visit to Toronto, of IRA sympathisers. On one occasion, she arrived, with her daughter, Lady Sarah Armstrong-Jones, for a performance of the Royal Ballet to persistent booing by eighty or so placard-waving hecklers. The problems of security were subsequently seen as so monumental that Princess Margaret cancelled a planned visit to the Shakespeare Theatre in Stratford, Ontario. Instead - and one could not have chosen a more diametrically opposite event - she visited a silver mine some 500 miles away where, dressed in scarlet overalls and a safety helmet, she was lowered 1,600 feet underground.

Most royals, however, take a fairly philosophical view of the more unpleasant aspects of their duties, whether at home or abroad, and the memory of the 1981 visit did not deter Princess Margaret from making a five-day tour of *Expo 86* in Vancouver, nor another brief visit to the Maritimes and Toronto in 1988. The show, after all, must go on.

ABOVE RIGHT: the Queen Mother at Osgoode Hall, Toronto in 1974 as a new honorary member of Upper Canada's Law Society. BELOW: over 25,000 saw her present colours to the Scottish Regiment at the C.N.E. Stadium. RIGHT: signing Montreal's Golden Book, watched by Mayor Drapeau. OPPOSITE PAGE, TOP: with an elderly couple outside Toronto's City Hall, and BOTTOM enthusiastic crowds see her arrive at Knox Presbyterian Church, Toronto.

114

'I LOST MY HEART…': THE GRACIOUS LOVE AFFAIR

Although Queen Elizabeth the Queen Mother was, many years after her 1939 tour of Canada with King George VI, to point out that 'during the darkest days of the War, my husband and I often recalled those happy times and found comfort in their recollection,' the King, regrettably, never saw Canada again. A post-War tour was arranged for 1951, but he was by then a man who, in Churchill's memorable words, 'walked with Death at his elbow' and, as we have seen, his daughter deputised for him that year. But, for his widow, that 1939 tour had become the beginning of a long, continuous and committed love-affair with Canada which has now lasted a full half-century. Not three years after the King's death, she was back, spending five days based in Ottawa, where she arrived by plane in weather as bitterly cold as her reception was enthusiastically warm. She had just completed some Canadian business in the United States, where at New York City's Canada Club she had unveiled a portrait of the new Queen Elizabeth II. The sight of this portrait was only one of several reminders of home. Because of this visit, for instance, she was unable to be in London for Prince Charles' sixth birthday, but he was thrilled to receive a transatlantic telephone call from her instead. Then, shortly before she was due to leave, she heard of the illness of her friend and former Lady-in-Waiting, Lavinia, Baroness Annaly - a great-aunt, in events, of the present Princess of Wales - and she rushed back to London to visit her. Sadly, it proved Lady Annaly's final illness, and she was dead within six months.

But that five-day visit to Ottawa was so replete with engagements and expanded so far outside the capital that it sparked off talk of the Queen Mother becoming the next Governor-General, a suggestion that took more serious form

two years later. It mirrored the speculation of a quarter of a century earlier when the Socialist Secretary of State for the Dominions received a proposal to make her husband, the then Duke of York, Governor-General and infuriated King George V by vetoing it on the grounds that 'the appointment of a royal Governor-General would make Canadians feel less democratic than the U.S.A.'

Speculation concerning the Queen Mother's possible appointment had effectively vanished by the time of her next visit to Canada, which consisted merely of brief stops in Vancouver and Montreal in January 1958, on her way back from Australasia and Honolulu. But in June 1962, she embarked on her first solo, full-scale, purpose-organised royal visit. The Black Watch (Royal Highland Regiment) had secured - and still retains - her services as its Colonel-in-Chief, and the Queen Mother flew to Montreal again to combine a regimental visit with the celebrations of the city's centenary. In presenting colours to the Regiment during a spectacular ceremony at McGill University, she recalled to the 18,000-strong audience the English assault on French-owned Montreal in 1760, and highlighted the march of the Regiment into the city to secure its capture. This, she said, was an example of 'the virtues of hardihood, courage and honour which crossed the sea from Scotland and made new history in

BELOW: in June 1979, the Queen Mother arrives at Woodbine Racetrack for the 120th Queen's Plate. OPPOSITE PAGE, TOP: addressing Canadians from Halifax at a televised inter-governmental dinner. BOTTOM: with officers of the Toronto Scottish Regiment at Fort York on the last day of her visit.

LEFT: the Duke of Kent enjoying a joke with Ontario's Lieutenant-Governor Pauline McGibbon after arriving in Toronto in March 1979 to visit the Lorne Scots Regiment. BELOW: delighted crowds watch the Queen Mother's reaction to having her hand unexpectedly seized and kissed by an admirer at Queen's Park, Toronto during her 1981 visit. BOTTOM: a word in your ear; the Queen Mother and Niagara-on-the-Lake's mayor at the town's 1981 bicentennial celebrations. OPPOSITE PAGE, BOTTOM LEFT: Mrs Louise Remy persuades one of her quadruplet daughters to put her clothes back on as the Queen Mother toured Toronto's Women's College Hospital.

helping to build this country.' As has become the case almost everywhere, the Queen Mother was rapturously received wherever she went: even Ottawans let their hair down when she visited their city - a reaction that would no doubt have astounded Princess Alice of Athlone - and even Ottawa's Mayor Charlotte Witton felt obliged to remark with more than a degree of admiration on the 'unwonted demonstrations' on the part of citizens who were 'usually comparably moved only by encounters in football and hockey, or by the excitement of our monster bingos.'

Three years later the Queen Mother attended the Scottish Regiment's jubilee in Toronto, and presented new colours. True to the form of her 1954 visit to Ottawa, this venture, conceived as a private postlude to an official visit to the West Indies, evolved into a five-day programme overflowing with engagements, many of which had little or nothing to do with the regiment she had come to visit. There was, for instance, a tour round Sunnybrook Hospital, where the Queen Mother amused onlookers by tickling the toes of a six-month-old baby, while an off-duty trip to the National Stud farm, with the industrialist E.P. Taylor, gave her the privilege of inspecting the Kentucky Derby winner, Northern Dancer, whose influence was soon to be felt in the Queen's own horse-breeding programme. But it seemed fitting that her presence in Toronto should be taken full advantage of, and they put on some sparkling banquets at which what one British Cabinet minister described as her 'large, cuddly and comfortable' presence was more than apt.

A slightly more prolonged visit was arranged in July 1967, when a two-week schedule took her to the Atlantic provinces of New Brunswick, Nova Scotia, Prince Edward Island and Newfoundland, and allowed her to complete her recuperation after an abdominal operation six months earlier. Seven years later, and with her visits abroad now noticeably rare, she was back yet again, to present new colours to each of her regiments in Toronto and Montreal. In the course of the seven-day visit, the Queen Mother went to Woodbine Park to see the Queen's Plate being run, and presented the traditional prize of fifty

ABOVE: three generations of the Royal Family in Canada as the Queen Mother joins her daughter, Princess Margaret and grand-daughter, Lady Sarah Armstrong-Jones before an Ontario Province dinner at the Royal York Hotel, Toronto, July 1981. RIGHT: Prince Michael of Kent arriving at Halifax for his 1984 four-day visit to Nova Scotia, and BELOW RIGHT signing the guest book at the Province House, with Premier John Buchanan.

OPPOSITE PAGE, TOP: a beaming Queen Mother on top of the world at the CN Tower on her 1985 visit to Toronto. BOTTOM LEFT: a breezy welcome from Scots bagpipers, and BOTTOM RIGHT the offer of a dog from an admirer in Toronto.

ABOVE: Princess Margaret touring the Canadian Pavilion at *Expo* 86 in Vancouver, and BELOW meeting elderly patients at the University of British Columbia Health Sciences Centre.

gold sovereigns to Jack Stafford, owner of the winning horse, Amber Herod. With her famous flair for appealing to young and old alike, she allowed children to touch and inspect her bouquet during a visit to Toronto's Sick Children's Hospital, and met a group of centenarians during the Dominion Day ceremonies at Queen's Park. She was also invested as an honorary member of the Law Society of Canada at Osgoode Hall - a rare privilege those days for a woman. And, as if her own engagements were not numerous enough, Prince Philip asked her to deputise for him in presenting awards to participators in the Duke of Edinburgh's Award Scheme who had successfully achieved the Gold Standard.

In 1979, the Queen Mother paid a week-long visit to Halifax and Toronto, attending the first international Gathering of Scottish clans in front of 9,000 people at Halifax's Metro Centre, meeting Mickey Mouse at the Canada Day celebrations, giving her first ever interview - to the *Toronto Star* - and being driven around in open carriages in spite of constant threats, demonstrations and potential dangers from sympathisers with the Irish Republican Army. The big event of the Halifax visit was her address to the government and people of the province, which was televised live from the Hotel Nova Scotian, while one of her better-publicised engagements in Toronto was her foray to the races at Woodbine Park to watch the 120th running of the Queen's Plate. She had first watched it in 1939, and three times since, and the rumours went round that many racegoers were putting additional money on one horse specifically because the Queen Mother had asked to have a second look at it!

Another visit to Ontario was carried out shortly before the wedding of Prince Charles and Lady Diana Spencer, when Niagara-on-the-Lake invited the Queen Mother to attend its bicentennial celebrations. Like the 1939 tour, this, too, was nearly cancelled - after Her Majesty slipped while climbing the stairs of the Horseguards building from which she was to have watched the Trooping the Colour ceremony in London the previous month. She grazed her leg, and the wound refused to heal and turned septic. Fortunately, though to this day she still wears a dressing on the graze, as she did when she arrived in Ottawa that July, the condition did not worsen nor force her to abandon either the Niagara festivities or the subsequent royal wedding. And no doubt she felt it was worth it. At Niagara itself, she had the great pleasure of meeting an 85-year-old lady, Winifred Gordon, who had emigrated to Canada in 1911 from a British orphanage, and who had seen the Queen Mother on her first visit over forty years before. Another, much younger, lady - one of the quadruplet toddlers born to Mrs Louise Remy - impressed the royal visitor in a rather different fashion by taking all her clothes off during an official tour of Toronto's Women's College Hospital! Then there was a family gathering when the Queen Mother met Princess Margaret and Lady Sarah Armstrong-Jones at a dinner given by the Premier of Ontario at the Royal York Hotel. And, of course, she couldn't resist yet another visit to Woodbine to watch the race for the Queen's Plate.

Which was precisely what she did again during her next visit in 1985, only on this occasion the rains had fallen long and hard during the previous days, and the walkway which the Queen Mother was due to take to join her waiting carriage was a ribbon of mud. So, in true Walter Raleigh tradition, the organisers built a long wooden platform over the route and covered it with red carpet, each section of it being held down by a muddy boot as the carpet-layers formed an unofficial guard of honour - much to the delighted appreciation of the royal visitor, who had a personal word of thanks for each of them. Previously that day, the Queen Mother had been scheduled to visit the CN Tower for the first time, but her hosts cancelled the event on the ground that the view from the top would be too hazy. The Queen Mother thought otherwise. She explained that she could see the top of the tower from her car, so by simple deduction, it should be possible to see the roadway at least from the top of the tower. Thus, just a few weeks short of her 85th birthday, she was whisked to the observation platform of the 1,850-foot tower for her first panoramic view of Toronto.

The Queen Mother's visit that year extended to Regina, where in a single day she travelled through four airports and two time zones, and enjoyed herself so much that, with her usual notorious unpunctuality, she was four hours late getting to her next stop, Edmonton. During a walkabout here, she was presented with a bouquet by a young boy who was confined to a wheelchair and who told her that he, too, was fond of flowers and wouldn't mind keeping one from her bouquet as a souvenir. So, naturally, she prised a flower free and gave it to him; he, just as naturally, raised his forearm in a victory salute to the crowds; and they, more naturally still, cheered both giver and receiver. Then, during a visit to a hospital for war veterans, where she was originally to have met only the usual token number of inmates, she prolonged her stay so that she could meet all of them personally. No matter that most of them were younger than she, nor that they were seated while she was on her feet: she was still a picture of alertness and warmth at the end of it all. And all that after having the

RIGHT: the Queen Mother, within two months of her 87th birthday, receives a loyal welcome at Uplands Airbase, Ottawa at the start of her tenth visit to Canada.

BELOW: admiring a superb view of Montreal from atop Mount Royal during a Sunday afternoon walkabout above the city.

previous night given a private party from which the last guest left at three in the morning!

At the end of her final, farewell lunch in Edmonton, at which her hosts presented her with a fine ceramic dish, expensively housed in green baize within a solid wooden box, she gave a short speech which was so well received that she used its key paragraph again, with suitable modifications, during her next visit in 1987. This journey centred around Montreal, with yet another renewal of regimental acquaintance with the Black Watch, who treated her to a grand display and march-past at the Percival Molson Memorial Stadium. The Queen Mother's well-chosen and touchingly delivered words reflected not only her satisfaction at being in the country on those occasions, but her gratification by her long association with Canada which had started almost half a century before. 'It is now some forty-six years,' she had said at Edmonton (she changed it to forty-eight years at Montreal),' since I first came to this country with the King in the anxious days shortly before the outbreak of the Second World War. I shall always look back on that visit with feelings of affection and happiness. I think I lost my heart to Canada - and to Canadians - then, and my feelings have not changed with the passage of time.'

Nor, for that matter, had the feelings of Canadians changed. Within six months of the end of her 1987 visit, she was invited back again for 1989!

LEFT: thirty years after last inspecting them, Princess Margaret, Colonel-in-Chief, presents a new colour to the Princess Louise Fusiliers, Halifax, July 1988. BELOW: touring the Nova Scotian fishing village of Sambro after unveiling a memorial there to local fishermen lost at sea.

CHAPTER SIX

'GOING HOME TO CANADA'

HAPPY RETURNS: A NEW NATION AND ITS SOVEREIGN

By the 1980s, the Queen and Prince Philip were old hands at visiting Canada. Following the patriation visit of 1982, there was a more subdued tone to the even briefer visit to Western Canada the following year. For all that, however, the British Columbians on that occasion proved themselves no slouches when, following a momentous, highly-publicised and eventful tour of America's west coast complete with its spectacular Hollywood settings, the Queen and Duke of Edinburgh stepped ashore at Victoria. Thousands of people had braved cold winds and drenching rain to give them a rousing welcome, and the Queen responded by seeming very much more at ease in this most British of Canadian environments after a strenuous and sometimes enervating American tour so replete with ostentatiously contrived festivity that at times she looked quite beyond surprise. Here in Canada, it was different. She was vastly amused to watch her equerry battling for supremacy over her umbrella which the wind had summarily blown inside out as they left Victoria's Legislature Building, and she took an almost childish pleasure in lighting a bonfire on a hill above the city as a symbolic guiding light to *Britannia* as the royal yacht glided out of Victoria for Vancouver.

The Queen's visit to Vancouver, like that to Victoria, was brief but busy. She and Prince Philip retraced Princess Margaret's steps to New Westminster and, like her, received a 21-anvil salute, and their biggest delight of a Beat-the-Clock day devoted to visiting as many small communities as possible, was the greeting accorded them by a flotilla of fibre-glass bathtubs at Nanaimo. Famed as the bathtub capital of the world, this tiny town, just 35 miles from Vancouver, has been holding bathtub races each year since 1967, and at the Queen's special request, no fewer than 27 of them, their outboard motors chugging furiously away, escorted the royal yacht in an hilarious mockery of protocol as she steamed across the Strait of Georgia.

But, as Prime Minister Trudeau reminded her, there was work to be done. The city made good use of the Queen's presence to promote its centennial celebration *Expo 86*, and the royal visitors were duly taken around the site of what later proved to be an enormous world fair. Its centrepiece was to be the $100 million Canadian Pavilion, structured in the form of a ship's prow with a roof of billowing sails, giving the whole an effect not dissimilar from the Sydney Opera House. Having shown the Queen and Prince Philip round the site, Mr

Trudeau unceremoniously said, 'Would you please do your work, Your Majesty?' whereupon the Queen pressed a button to activate the pouring of the first delivery of concrete into the building's reinforcing caissons. Later, at a spectacular rally in which 7,000 schoolchildren formed a single, huge choir, the Queen relayed to 161 countries a message which had travelled 5,000 miles across Canada by air, road, rail and ferry to reach her for the occasion: 'As Queen of Canada, I would like to extend to all peoples of the world an invitation from the people of Canada to visit the world exposition, which will take place in Vancouver in 1986.' She could have added a personal guarantee that the British Columbians would prove more than just adequate hosts: as she left Vancouver for home, she assured Mr Trudeau that after only three days in the province, '*Britannia* looks like a floating flower-shop'.

Within eighteen months, the Queen and Prince Philip were back for a much longer tour for which the preparations turned out to be much more protracted and problematical than usual. Scheduled to begin in mid-July of that year, it was put in jeopardy by the resignation of Mr Trudeau the previous month and the strong possibility of a general election, so timed by a combination of political opportunism and constitutional necessity that the campaign leading up to it could not avoid clashing with the Queen's presence in the country. Rarely had the balance of political convenience and royal precedence been so hotly disputed in Canada. Buckingham Palace made it immediately clear that the Queen would not visit during an election campaign for fear of appearing to favour the party of her constitutional hosts. Their political rivals, the Conservatives under Brian Mulroney, were quick to make an issue out of it. 'Rudely interrupt the Queen's visit,' said one, 'and then let's see what the people of Canada think.' 'It will be an outrage,' said another, 'to put off for political gain an event which has been so eagerly awaited, and on which so many people have worked for so long.'

The Liberals, under their new leader, John Turner, were conscious of the potential loss of popular goodwill if the visit were postponed, and attempted an accommodation by which the Queen would visit Canada as one of her kingdoms, even during the campaign, provided she avoided Ottawa and contact with federal leaders no matter what their political hue. A prolonged official silence caused unease, frustration and eventually annoyance. In Britain, where it was widely imagined that the Queen had been kept totally in the dark, the *Daily Telegraph* argued that the situation should not have reached 'the point where the Queen, who has burdens of her own, is made to appear as maid-in-waiting to political

OPPOSITE: all smiles as the Queen accepts a bouquet from four-year-old Erin Johnson at City Hall, Victoria in March 1983.

opportunism. That does not dignify Canada,' it concluded: 'it is really a matter not of politics, but of manners.'

Eventually, and within five days of the scheduled start of the tour, Mr Turner flew to London to ask the Queen to postpone. Conscious of her strict constitutional duties, 'with regret and in the knowledge that so many Canadians have been looking forward to expressing their loyalty and affection to Her Majesty,' as the Buckingham Palace statement somewhat immodestly ran, she agreed. There was an immediate storm of protest and dismay, in which the Conservatives, sensing the makings of electoral victory out of an arguable discourtesy to the Queen, predicted that Mr Turner 'will have

to answer before the Canadian people' - a threat which the Liberal leader embraced with resignation. 'If it costs me some support, then I am prepared to take it, he countered. Other expressions of annoyance were voiced by tour organisers, one of whom angrily ridiculed the postponement 'just so a politician could win votes', while the minister of the Trinity Anglican Church in Cornwall, Ontario, which the Queen was scheduled to visit, thought it 'disgraceful that a politician puts his own personal ambitions ahead of the needs of his peoples.'

The problems created by the postponement of the tour were enormous, as was the consequent expenditure of time, money and sheer human resources. Every town and community had its story of upheaval and disappointment, the cumulative effect of which resulted in a shower of mind-boggling statistics. Ontario, for instance, estimated a bill of tens of thousands of dollars for revised invitations and programmes alone. In every host province, plaques which the Queen was due to have unveiled had all to be recast to show new dates. The Hotel

OPPOSITE PAGE, TOP: in Toronto in 1980, Princess Alexandra visits the Grace Baker Health Centre, and BOTTOM cuts the Queen's

Own Canadian Rifles' 120th birthday cake. BELOW: the Queen at the Patriation banquet at Rideau Hall in April 1982.

Beauséjour at Moncton, where she was to have stayed, had to lay off the extra staff it had engaged, and sell at absurdly reduced prices the huge amount of extra food it had ordered - all in anticipation of a full book of reservations - and it suffered a loss of $25,000 as a result. Manitoba likewise took a financial hammering and promptly decided to send its own bill of claim direct to the federal government who equally promptly assured the province that it had no plans for compensation. Worst hit and most sorely disappointed were those involved in events which could not be delayed or re-scheduled - the opening of the Martin Goodman Trail in Toronto, an inter-faith service at the city's Varsity Stadium, horse-racing at the Woodbine racetrack, the opening of Dinsdale Park at Brandon, Manitoba. And because of prearranged early Autumn duties in Cyprus and Egypt, the Duke of Edinburgh's presence in Canada, once the royal visit might eventually be re-scheduled, became a matter of increasing doubt. In the event, he was obliged to cancel a whole sheaf of accepted invitations in Manitoba, and leave the Queen to carry out that leg of the tour by herself.

By late September, when the royal visit eventually began, however, the bitterness surrounding its postponement seemed to have been forgotten. The tour was essentially celebratory in nature and purpose, with rarely a town, city or province on the royal itinerary lacking some birthday or other to fete. The Conservatives had been voted into office, the Queen had in the meantime experienced the joy of becoming a grandmother for the fourth time with the birth of Prince Harry, and the glow of satisfaction on all sides that the tour was at last underway seemed well reflected by the unusually warm weather which greeted the royal couple as they arrived in New

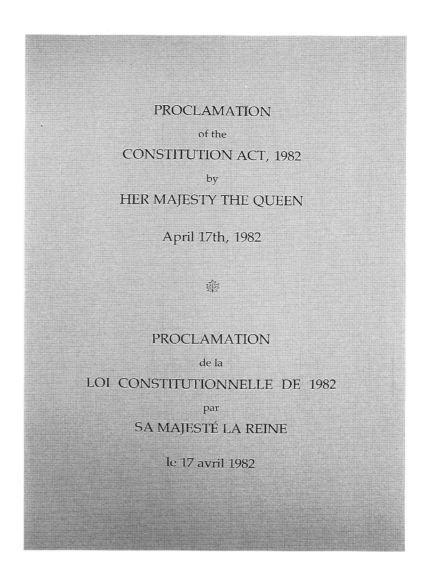

PROCLAMATION
of the
CONSTITUTION ACT, 1982
by
HER MAJESTY THE QUEEN

April 17th, 1982

PROCLAMATION
de la
LOI CONSTITUTIONNELLE DE 1982
par
SA MAJESTÉ LA REINE

le 17 avril 1982

'The end of a long winter… and the beginning of a new spring,' was how Prime Minister Trudeau described the signing by the Queen of the 1982 Constitution Act OPPOSITE PAGE, TOP, for which she made a special four-day visit to Ottawa. During her stay, she also inaugurated the East block of the Legislature complex OPPOSITE PAGE, BOTTOM, which had been newly renovated over the previous four years. The weather on the day of the ceremonial signing of the new Act was not the most clement but, accompanied by Mr Trudeau BELOW, the Queen made her way into the streets of Ottawa to meet the crowds who welcomed both her and the new Constitution with equal enthusiasm. RIGHT: a happy Queen waving to crowds while inspecting a guard of honour at the Legislature buildings in Victoria in March 1983.

Brunswick. Here were brilliant blue skies, cloudless backdrops to the blazing reds and yellows of an Acadian fall. A summer visit might have proved warmer, but September in her best welcoming mood certainly offered compensations.

'Better late than never,' reflected the Queen at the first State banquet of the tour, and the little fishing community of Shediac proved her point with a simple and touching display of loyalty. The Queen was there primarily to visit its parish of St Joseph and to unveil a new plaque at the comparatively new church - a round, modern edifice of whitewashed brick - which bears its name. A much older link with the past manifested itself when 102-year-old Mrs Leonie Williams handed the Queen the official bouquet: she told Her Majesty that, as a teenager, she had watched HMS *Ophir* sail round the Maritime Provinces carrying the Duke and Duchess of York in October 1901, and that thirty-eight years later, she stood patiently at the side of a railroad track, waving her Union Jack and shouting 'Vive le Roi; vive la Reine' as King George VI and Queen Elizabeth glided by on that famous blue and silver train. Later that day, a more cosmopolitan Moncton seemed to be making amends for the Queen's abbreviated Balmoral holiday by putting on an outdoor entertainment at Victoria Park that included a fine display of Highland dancing where swords glistened, bagpipes blew and kilts flew. Then Fredericton, named after George III's second son, who was born two months after the province was first colonised by British subjects, offered the Queen and Prince Philip the elegance of its charming streets and parklands and the formal privilege of 'augmenting her arms in right of New Brunswick'. By this ceremony, the city of stately elms has for over half a decade already boasted a colourful new crest topped by a leaping salmon royally crowned. The festive mood was

ABOVE: *Britannia* arrives at Vancouver Harbour from Victoria. BELOW: the Queen gathering daffodils from children at the University of British Columbia. OPPOSITE PAGE: June 1983; the Prince and Princess of Wales' first Canadian tour.

TOP: Diana with crowds at the Garrison Grounds, Halifax, and inspecting with Prince Charles BOTTOM RIGHT a montage of flags. BOTTOM LEFT: a rainy walkabout at Halifax Commons.

perpetuated that night by a dazzling display of pyrotechnics which the royal party watched from the balcony of the Hotel Beauséjour following a State dinner, and by a late-hour meeting with nine-month-old Daniel Val Leblanc, New Brunswick's very first bicentennial baby, who at nine o'clock that night was only just sufficiently awake to respond to what might well turn out to be the most distinguished event of his whole life.

After a brief, and rather stiffly formal visit to Ottawa, the Queen and Duke of Edinburgh joined the Royal Yacht *Britannia* at Morrisburg for a succession of visits up the St Lawrence Seaway (a quarter of a century after she had opened it) to call - in a stop-go progress encompassing four visits in ten hours - on a string of settlements which owe both origin and identity to two centuries of intense and unbroken loyalty to the Crown. It was a pilgrimage to acknowledge and, no doubt, perpetuate that loyalty: a visit to a Cornwall church founded on land granted by George III in 1819; an historical treat in the form of a delightful and instructive pageant at Prescott in which the old post-Revolution fighting days were re-created with incredible authenticity and local colour; the inauguration of the Loyalist Parkway at Amherstview by the opening of gates hinged to pillars bearing the royal cyphers of George III and Elizabeth II; and a moving visit to the Loyalist Mohawk site nearby, where the Indians re-enacted their ancestors' landing as fugitives from the rebelling colonies across the water. The royal schedule had overrun by this time, and dusk was falling as the Indians sang the Queen a hymn. In the darkness beyond glowed the lights of *Britannia*, waiting in silhouette to receive the royal party aboard at the end of a long day. As if suddenly reminded by the sight of her home base, the Queen rose during the beautifully-intoned hymn and made her way, amid the applause of the crowds, to the royal barge. They were still singing as it struck out from the waterside: a heartfelt, ethereal and magical accompaniment to a short royal journey by water, and born of the kind of intense, unquestioning loyalty that must surely mark the events of that day in the Queen's memory for life.

The Loyalist act is invariably difficult to follow, particularly with the Queen, for whom it must have served as the highest form of flattery - and with royalty, as Disraeli once said, you have to lay flattery on with a trowel! But Toronto, where the Queen and Prince Philip arrived two days later, celebrated its

own sesquicentenary with verve and éclat. There were mighty, ceremonial salutes and presentations as they bowled into Queen's Park in a State landau, bagpipe tributes from Ontario's police, a fly-past of modern and heritage aircraft at the Air Force Memorial, a rousing, strident welcome for 'La Regina' from the Italian community where grape-crushing displays and the singing of ballads about donkeys and drunkards provided entertainment of a different sort. A superb military spectacle at the Exhibition Stadium that evening, reckoned the largest of its kind in Canada's entire history, combined pageantry, thrills, music and fireworks on the grandest of scales, but very nearly went wrong. As the Queen, swathed in mink against the night chill, arrived in the State landau, the noise of the 21-gun salute startled the two leading horses; they shied, panicked and turned about-face, to bring an otherwise magnificent procession to an embarrassing halt. Grooms and horse-guards were quick to untangle the tack, but by then other horses had become fretful, and the firing of the cannon was wisely brought to an end. In the ensuing efforts to keep the show going, perhaps Toronto could at least claim another 'first' - the only Canadian city to have given the Queen an eight-gun salute!

A salute of a different kind took place at Windsor the following day, when the Queen discovered that President Reagan was visiting Detroit at the same time. She took the opportunity of exchanging greetings with him as she returned to Toronto that evening, expressing her delight 'to learn that, metaphorically speaking, we were only divided today by a strip of water between our two countries'. To which Mr Reagan replied, 'We are pleased that nothing more than water separates our countries, and pray it shall always be thus. Nancy and I wish you the very best, and hope that your visit will be a happy one.'

It is a mark of major royal visits to Canada that minority communities enjoy a substantial share of their sovereign's attentions, and the loyalties of the Indians, in spite of their long-standing grievances over land rights and self-government, have always been well rewarded. The Six Nations Mohawks secured the Queen's presence at Brantford, Ontario for the dedication of their newly-restored chapel on its two-hundredth

ABOVE: a sparkling Princess Diana arrives for a State banquet given by the Prime Minister in Halifax, at which Mr Trudeau LEFT spoke glowingly of her qualities. OPPOSITE PAGE, TOP LEFT: loyalist Shelburne gave a warm and vigorous welcome to the Waleses, who were shown other reminders of days gone by BOTTOM PICTURE at Bridgewater. TOP RIGHT: Prince Charles takes the Salute at a march-past at Saint John át the beginning of the New Brunswick stage of the tour.

birthday. Their host, Chief Wellington Staats, reminded the Queen that his people 'sacrificed everything, including our homeland, for ties with the British monarchy', ties which were all too evident by the display of royal gifts dating back to 1786, stained glass windows bearing the present Queen's own cypher, and the fact that the chapel was given royal status by Edward VII in 1904.

The touching simplicity of this informal visit was reflected during the Manitoba stage of the tour. As if to emphasise the fact that this was the Queen's first visit to the province for almost fifteen years, Premier Pawley gave the Queen a history book of all royal visits there; and the multi-cultural tradition which has grown up in 'Friendly Manitoba' delighted the

Queen when displays of Ukrainian, Scottish, Indian and French entertainment filled her hours at Dauphin, while she ate decorously from a picnic basket full of traditional ethnic delicacies like pickled cherries and mushrooms, cinnamon butterhorns, canapés of sausage and ham, smoked tongue, cheeses and fruits. At a vintage fashion show at Dugald, she was quietly amused by the nostalgic mélange of fox furs, cloche hats, lace-frilled dresses, bustled skirts, precariously balanced toques and, almost as a reminder of the Duchess of Connaught, a thick, woollen Edwardian skating outfit, complete with large feathered hat and ermine stole!

The Queen experienced a reminder of even earlier times at St Boniface, when her hosts re-created the landing, exactly 250 years before, of La Vérendrye at Fort Maurepas to found the first trading post on the Red River. On a murky day reminiscent, perhaps, of the weather La Vérendrye himself might have experienced, the Queen watched as eight canoes advanced up river, bearing almost a hundred men dressed in Voyageur costume. With bagpipe music drifting eerily from their craft, they cheered themselves ashore. The Queen went to greet them, doubtless flattered by the attentions of these burly adventurers, and certainly somewhat amused by their leader, Justice Monnin, who played one of La Vérendrye's four sons, as he doffed his coyote-fur cap and offered to act as her guide during a long walkabout among huge crowds.

That night, she took her official leave of Canada - for the fifteenth time - and looked back on her fortnight's tour as 'a wonderful experience'. Her sixteenth, and most recent visit began in the autumn of 1987, with a journey to Vancouver where she was to preside over the Commonwealth heads of Government meetings. 'Preside' is not quite the right word, since the meetings themselves are conducted in her absence. But the week-long conference embraces the statement that she is Head of the Commonwealth by her insistence on being present during many of the non-political events. Thus, at her headquarters in the Four Seasons Hotel, she met each of the Commonwealth leaders individually for twenty minutes each during five separate morning or afternoon sessions - a total discussion time of no less than fifteen hours. She hosted them in groups of fifteen to three separate lunches, and headed a magnificent banquet for the entire delegation, following a reception at which she was photographed surrounded by all forty-five of them. As luck would have it, the Conference was taking place on the heels of Fiji's departure from the Commonwealth following a nationalist coup, and the Queen spent some time during the dinner putting the finishing touches to a speech in which reference to the event, whereby the interests of the immigrant Indian majority were being prejudiced by the indigenous Fijian minority, had had to be

ABOVE: Charles and Diana listen to a local school orchestra at Rothesay. BELOW: leaving All Saints' Church, St Andrews-by-sea, N.B. after Sunday morning service. ABOVE LEFT: with the Governor-General and Prime Minister at Rideau Hall, Ottawa, where OPPOSITE PAGE Diana found herself swamped by crowds on Parliament Hill.

'Share the Spirit' was the message of the people on St. John's Day, who were celebrating the 400th anniversary of Newfoundland's capital. Prince Charles and his wife did just that. ABOVE LEFT: the Prince giving an address at Canada Games Park and, with the Princess, being welcomed through an arch LEFT noticeably different in composition from that through which Edward, Prince of Wales had entered the city back in 1919. ABOVE: the royal couple at the historic site of Cape Spear National Park, which contains Newfoundland's oldest lighthouse. OPPOSITE PAGE: Diana enjoys a rapturous reception from the people of Charlottetown, towards the end of their 1983 tour.

hastily inserted. In the result, her words were a masterpiece of diplomacy and firmness. 'I have been greatly saddened,' she announced, 'by recent events in Fiji and I am sure that all the members of the Commonwealth will share my feelings. I know that you will join with me in praying for the future peace and happiness of all the people of Fiji, whatever their race or origins.'

While the Queen was attending to Commonwealth business, Prince Philip, who has rarely failed to accompany her on any of her many tours abroad, carved out his own programme - a visit to the Seaforth Highlanders, a presentation and dinner in connection with the Award Scheme, a tour of HMCS *Saskatchewan* at Esquimault, a visit to the British Columbia Provincial Museum in Victoria and so on. Perhaps the two most rewarding events for him - in addition to the brass band welcome and customary wardroom gin at *Esquimault* - were his visit to the Sail and Life Training Society's schooner *Robertson II*, where he saw young people being trained to rig and operate the nineteenth century craft as an exercise in teamwork; and the day he spent whalewatching off Vancouver Island, a most successful venture organised by WWF Canada, in which an endless succession of killer whales showed up as if they knew instinctively what turns royalty on!

Eventually, the Queen and Prince Philip left Vancouver, though not before a couple of incidents took the Queen by surprise. One was the rather premature fall of a curtain

concealing a new coat of arms which she was to have unveiled at the Law Courts. The Queen had been given the electronic pad on which to press the button, but it proved rather too sensitive, and the curtain fell abruptly and rather dramatically before she had even applied the royal finger. Slightly taken aback, she made light of the mishap by pretending that the pad was giving off electric shocks and, much to the delight of both officials and onlookers, withdrew her finger smartly. The second incident involved the Queen being stopped in her tracks - for the first time in her life - by a reporter anxious to question her about developments in the Fiji question. She replied patiently and tactfully to his enquiries, until he asked whether it was true that she was going to make a further public statement on the matter. 'Ah!' she said, as if she held some close secret and was determined to keep it that way - and as she did so, turned neatly and non-committally aside to continue on her way.

The royal couple's next stop was in Saskatchewan. Few of the Queen's tours of Canada have been complete without some reference to ethnic communities, and the Saskatchewan leg of this tour was replete with reminders of Canada's multi-national heritage. At Wanuskewin, the Queen drew back a buffalo hide to unveil a commemorative stone inaugurating the Canadian government's $6 million development of the newly discovered archaeological site of an original Cree tribal meeting place, and she watched an outdoor display of Indian dances and singing in such glacial conditions that she kept a substantial plaid rug wrapped round her legs. Then, at Canora, she attended a demonstration of Ukrainian folk songs and dances in the local curling rink, and was offered the traditional gift of bread and salt as she entered the former home - now a prayer-house - of Peter Verigen who, in 1899, had led thousands of Ukrainians out of Tsarist Russia with the financial help of Tolstoy and the promise of a grant of Canadian land by Queen Victoria. At the house, the Queen met the daughters of some of those settlers, for whom Russian is still the first language, and she heard them serenade her with Russian songs from the building's verandah as she left. She referred light-heartedly to the pioneering story at Kindersley, where she met grain and cattle farmers who had built up their livelihood from the pioneering beginnings of recent generations. 'The first European settlers arrived in this part of the country not much more than a hundred years ago,' she told them. 'Prince Philip and I came here thirty-six years ago, so we can almost claim to be pioneers.'

And, like a latter-day pioneer herself, she made for what in many ways was the climax of her tour - a return, after twenty-three long years, to the city of Quebec. Considering that, at the time of her last visit there, and for many years since, the Québecois had been all for severing their ties with the monarchy, this was no mean achievement, though it should be emphasised that it came about not so much as the result of the Queen's influence, but only after long and arduous negotiations between the national government, the provincial governments and Quebec province - negotiations which finally resolved that the province should be an autonomous region within the constitution of Canada. The accord has not pleased everyone, but hatchets had been sufficiently deeply buried for the Queen to be able to renew her acquaintance with this charming city, much of which is virtually unchanged since the eighteenth century when it was bitterly fought for between the French and the British.

Indeed, relations between the Queen and the Québecois seemed as warm and friendly as if nothing had intervened since the good old days of the Fifties, and there was a general feeling that all concerned were anxious to make up lost time. The crowds were quiet, curious - almost as if they did not know how to handle a royal walkabout - and polite, and while it was Quebec flags, not Union Jacks, that were flown from poles and windows, waved by thousands of children, and hung below the welcoming trumpets, it was clear, both in the city and in the various communities along the lower St Lawrence River, which she also visited, that the royal couple were back in favour. They named a park and a square after the Queen, proudly showed her an exhibition of children's paintings depicting life at Buckingham Palace, and took the Duke to Cap Tourmente nature reserve to witness the absorbing spectacle of a massive flock of snow geese clouding the skies on their way to winter in the southern USA.

The Queen returned the compliment, freely recognising Quebec's new status, giving most of her speeches in French, and insisting on carrying out a full inspection of the Vingt-Deuxième - the only French-speaking Canadian regiment (and of which she is Colonel-in-Chief) - despite a surprise fall of snow which threatened to curtail the ceremony. And on her final night, she looked back on three and a half decades of her own royal visits to Canada. 'Tomorrow,' she mused, 'we will be leaving Canada after our sixteenth visit since we first landed on Canadian soil in Montreal in 1951. We shall go with memories of the warmth and kindness of the people, and deeply impressed by the progress which has been so evident wherever we have been.' It was the Queen's customarily reticent way of saying that she'd had a great time.

LEFT: the Prince and Princess of Wales dressed for the part at the reconstructed site of Fort Edmonton, during the Klondike Days barbecue and musical entertainment that awaited them in Alberta. 'It may not be in the best royal tradition,' said one of the hosts, 'but it beats the hell out of tree-planting!' BELOW LEFT: Diana accepts an official bouquet from a young resident of Montague, Prince Edward Island. BELOW: Prince Charles, robed for the occasion, speaking to members of Alberta University after having been awarded an honorary doctorate of laws. OPPOSITE PAGE: the royal couple acknowledging the cheers of 70,000 people in the streets of Edmonton.

DIANA AND DI-MANIA: A PRINCESS FOR THE PEOPLE

After the major constitutional issues of the Sixties and Seventies had been settled, the Eighties, as we have seen, began to witness a renewal of the happy times traditionally associated with royal visits to Canada. Rarely was a better example of the generations-old mutual admiration between Canada and the Royal Family demonstrated than during the 17-day tour undertaken by the most celebrated married couple in the world today, the Prince and Princess of Wales, in 1983. Following their exuberant wedding in 1981, the much heralded and long-awaited birth of their first child, and son and heir, Prince William in 1982, and their first joint Commonwealth

visit a year later, this young, much feted couple were at the very height of their world-wide popularity. It was thus with something bordering on delirium that Canadians heard that the tour of their country, originally arranged for a time which the Princess' pregnancy in events rendered inappropriate, would take place in June 1983, and embrace the Maritime Provinces, Ottawa and Alberta. Any feeling, as the date of the tour's beginning neared, that the phenomenal success of the Waleses' Australasian visit would leave the journey to Canada devoid of novelty or excitement for either the royal visitors or their hosts failed to take into account the Canadians' well-

known taste for celebration and inventiveness and the almost unquestioning loyalty of Canada's multicultural citizens.

It was, *par excellence*, a visit to the people, no matter how officially its programme was devised. There were, of course, buildings to open, plaques to unveil, saplings to plant and speeches to make - such are the necessary accoutrements of the royal round. But above all, the royal progress provided an unprecedented opportunity for a conscientious yet personable Prince and his dazzlingly popular wife to make brief, informal contact with the people who comprise the nation. They graced the smallest communities with their presence, affording both adults and children the memories of a lifetime with a hand firmly shaken, a conversation snatched out of nothing, flowers and presents accepted with such surprised delight that they might have been the last thing a royal visitor expects to receive on a walkabout, and for the really lucky ones, a quick kiss from the world's most adored princess. Charles and Diana also lent that elusive brand of royal distinction and purpose to the great occasion - those glittering banquets, those massive open-air parties, those national celebrations - with a combination of style and naturalness that had a lot of the less outgoing, rather more indifferent Canadians thinking again about the value of their passivity.

The tour made 1983 a high point in the relationship between the Crown and its Canadian subjects. In the course of their itinerary, the royal couple were feted by Empire Loyalists, French Acadians, Micmac Indians and visitors from the States, as well as by descendants of old British stock and nineteenth and twentieth-century immigrants from Europe. Right from the start, Di-mania became a household word. In Halifax, screaming, frantic women hoisted high their Union Jacks and virtually drowned the welcoming proceedings with their noise; at Saint John, New Brunswick, both teenagers and older women were overwhelmed in the

ABOVE LEFT: the Queen meets 102-year-old Mrs Leonie Williams at Shediac, N.B. at the beginning of her delayed tour of 1984.
ABOVE: signing the warrant to augment the province's coat-of-arms, Fredericton.
OPPOSITE PAGE, TOP: an indulgent reaction from Prince Philip as a little girl suddenly turns tail after presenting flowers to the Queen. BOTTOM: the Queen's scarlet outfit complements the blaze of red from the Mounties' uniforms as she and the Duke arrive in Ottawa.

heady atmosphere of mass hysteria, and dissolved helplessly into tears. As, indeed, did one young boy in Ottawa, who impulsively rushed up to Diana and kissed her. 'I can't believe I just did that,' he blurted through his tears afterwards. Shouts of 'We want Di' echoed from every direction, no matter where the royal couple went. Posters showing official portraits of the Princess were waved from side to side or jigged up and down above a sea of heads, along with hand-made banners proclaiming love and loyalty. One in St John announced simply, 'We love you. Give our love to little William and the rest of the family.'

There was certainly an official form of Di-mania, too. Even Prime Minister Trudeau - noted, sometimes reviled, for his less than traditionally respectful demeanour in the company of royalty - fairly folded before Her Majesty's daughter-in-law at a dinner in Ottawa. Speaking to Prince Charles, he put forward the frankly preposterous suggestion that 'if by exception the Government of Canada could enlist you into a job, we would like you to become the chief guide of Her Highness. The pay you would not find very high, but the company would be very pleasant.' One of his provincial counterparts, New Brunswick's Richard Hatfield, went one better - or worse? - at a dinner in Saint John. Speaking out

against a barrage of newspaper speculation that had dogged the Prince and Princess since their wedding, he called out, 'We have heard and read the lies. Today it is wonderful to meet and know the truth. It's my turn to propose a toast. In doing so, I say: Let the flame burn, to warm hope, to cancel cynicism and despair, to heat the soul that remains and remembers. Yes, let the flame burn. For the flame is love. I ask you to join with me in a toast to love - the Prince and Princess of Wales.'

Everyone present became acutely embarrassed at such an unprecedented outpouring. Prince Charles' mouth went into an involuntary spasm, while his wife giggled in disbelief that this could be happening to her. Hatfield, a deeply committed monarchist in a way that Trudeau never was, denied later that he was drunk - except on the Princess' charm - and blamed his rambling eulogy on the fact that 'I am not articulate.' Yet his words flew round the world, attracting for him the instant fame - or notoriety - of one who, amongst thousands of

OPPOSITE PAGE, TOP: the Queen of Canada with her new Cabinet, September 1984. At Rideau Hall, Her Majesty sits with new Prime Minister Mulroney and his two-week-old Cabinet, beneath portraits of herself and the Duke of Edinburgh. RIGHT: leaving Morrisburg's Crysler Park Marina by royal barge, to join *Britannia* for a series of visits to riverside settlements. OPPOSITE PAGE, BOTTOM: the royal visitors watching part of a huge display of historic regimental warfare at Fort Wellington, Prescott, Ontario. BELOW RIGHT: the Queen and Prince Philip in Dieppe Park, Windsor, where they were welcomed not only by Windsor citizens, but also by American visitors from Detroit, whose city can be seen just across the lake. TOP: the Queen with Ukrainian folk dancers at the Selo Ukraina Amphitheatre at Dauphin, Manitoba; she is holding a bouquet of traditional Ukrainian flowers.

anonymous admirers, had quite simply succumbed in public against all behavioural logic to the magnetism of a girl still only twenty-one years old.

More serious consequences of Di-mania attended the opening by Prince Charles of the Police Headquarters building in Ottawa, as scores of people in the crowd of 10,000 keeled over in midsummer temperatures which reached 86 degrees. The Prince himself remarked, on opening the building, that 'its first use will probably be as a first aid post.' He also had a mischievously witty response to one French Acadian who told him that he had been to London for the royal wedding. 'Were you really?' replied the Prince, no doubt rather bucked by the compliment. 'That was very rash of you. You didn't get over-charged, did you?' Sometimes it seemed as if Diana could not cope with all the adulation. At a welcoming banquet in Halifax, she received a standing ovation as she entered the room, but was unable to acknowledge it save by an embarrassed lowering of the head. At one stop during a walkabout in Saint John, it seemed as if she were struggling to shake hands with almost everybody in the 40,000-strong crowd! Prince Charles became visibly anxious about her and, after speaking to his entourage, decided to prompt her to speed things up a bit. The pace quickened, though probably much against Diana's will. When, at Shearwater, a 91-year-old woman told her, 'You must get tired of meeting so many people and shaking so many hands', Diana replied, 'Oh no, not at all. I love it.' She may have gritted her teeth as she said it, but it showed at least that she had come to terms with royalty's unofficial motto: Never Complain!

The tour was tailor-made for getting the best from the royal visitors. They were taken on a boat trip down the Rideau Canal at Ottawa; they were treated to a lobster lunch at Bridgewater - at which Diana refused to wear a bib and tucker because she feared it would not go over her hat without knocking it askew; Prime Minister Trudeau hosted her and Prince Charles at a barbecue at his country home, and in casual gear they wandered around the grounds, eating from plates of smoked salmon and corn cobs. There were children's sing-songs during the many musical performances they heard,

though Diana usually looked rather conspicuous as she half-heartedly joined in the singing; and there was, following the success of Princess Margaret's involvement in the Edmonton proceedings three years earlier, a repeat of that superb Klondike-style entertainment, in which Diana entranced the invited guests in her high-Victorian ensemble of peaches-and-cream satins and silks, high boots, bustled skirt, whale-boned bodice, parasol, and a dainty, flowered saucer hat to cover her otherwise rather obvious twentieth-century hairstyle. And to complete the happy picture, thousands of balloons soared into the skies in Diana's honour, both at Halifax, and again at Edmonton, where 65,000 people assembled at the Commonwealth Stadium for the World University Games and sang *Happy Birthday To You* - even though there were still two days to go before her 22nd birthday!

As everyone had long since come to expect, it was a tour for individuals as well as for crowds, and incidents both delightful and mildly embarrassing came thick and fast. At Edmonton, the little girl who presented Diana with the official bouquet persisted in walking with her through the main street, determined to tail her through her entire walkabout, until at last someone persuaded her that, in the nicest possible way, her services were no longer required. At Halifax a 12-year-old boy asked to kiss Diana's hand, and was awestruck immediately afterwards. 'Boy! Is she beautiful!' he sighed. 'I just had to do that.' And Diana herself just had to let a four-year-old blind boy 'see' her by touch, and allowed him to pass his hand over her face, hair, shoes and legs during a special private audience, after she had received a bunch of flowers from him earlier in the day without realising his disability.

BELOW: the Queen responding to Premier William Davis' welcome at Ontario's bicentennial dinner in Toronto. RIGHT: the Queen and Prince Philip with Chief Wellington Staats at the Six Nations Indians Chapel near Brantford, Ontario. OPPOSITE PAGE: the Queen in the Winnipeg area. TOP: at St Boniface after watching a re-enactment of the La Vérendrye landings. BOTTOM: at the Costume Museum at Dugald.

At Ottawa, a waiter at a State banquet distinguished himself by forgetting to fill Diana's glass with champagne for the Loyal Toast; while, after a dinner in Saint John, the New Brunswick Premier was equally forgetful about calling for the saying of the Grace until his royal guests were on their way out! When he did remember, he stopped so suddenly that Prince Charles bumped into him and was knocked against a door post. On top of all that, there were extremes of weather that caught the royal party napping once or twice. The high summer heat of the nation's capital was 40 degrees up on the blowy climate of the Maritimes, though one got the impression that Diana definitely preferred the latter. Never one to stand high temperatures easily, she complained of the heat in Ottawa, adding, while talking to a couple of girls in the crowd who were wearing swimsuits, 'You're wearing the right equipment. I wish I could wear something like that.'

As always, the Prince and Princess were swamped with presents, and no article was too trivial to be treasured. Least romantic of all, but as well received as any, was a family set of three coat-hangers which an anonymous hand thrust towards Diana during a walkabout. Scores of others were loaded into her arms for Prince William, and at almost every port of call there were official gifts for him too. A deerskin Indian suit from the Micmac tribe at Charlo - 'Perfect!' said Diana. 'William will love it.' A model fishing boat from Shelburne. A canoe from St Andrew's. A rocking-horse from the inhabitants of Prince Edward Island. Scores of items of clothing. Hundreds of toys. The list was endless.

There was no indication that the Canadians were put out at not having been favoured with the young Prince's presence amongst them, which had so cheered the Australians and New Zealanders a few months earlier. But there was disappointment, and Prince Charles had to be ready with explanations. 'We felt that the ship's voyage might not be good for him,' he reasoned, rather vaguely, 'and that life aboard the Royal Yacht might not have suited him.' Diana was quick to let her own maternal feelings show. Hardly had she landed in Nova Scotia that she was confessing, 'I miss him very much. I'm sorry we couldn't bring him this time, but,' she added rashly and, in events, untruthfully, 'we will next time.' She was missing him even more by the time she got to Ottawa, according to one woman to whom she also revealed, 'He's a beautiful boy and we are both extremely proud of him.'

William's first birthday, which fell at the end of the first week of the tour while his parents were in Ottawa, gave the Canadians another excuse for celebration. Diana was again overwhelmed with presents for him, and special birthday greetings were spread across banners everywhere. Prince Charles had regretted earlier that he could not disclose what he and Diana had bought William for his birthday, but he gave the crowds a clue. 'Something he won't be able to break,' he told them, with more than a little hint of his son's tearaway nature. Very early on the day itself, the Prince and Princess were up and about, putting through a telephone call to Kensington Palace, where young William was busy ploughing through piles of other gifts. 'All I could hear were a few squeaks,' Prince Charles later reported to walkabout crowds

Prince Andrew spent eight days in the Maritimes during the summer of 1985. ABOVE RIGHT: preparing for the helicopter flight from Saint John, New Brunswick, to Sussex. RIGHT: on a cruise along the Saint John River. OPPOSITE PAGE, TOP: with youngsters in the crowd at Fredericton. BOTTOM: watching athletics at Saint John's Canada Games Stadium.

in the capital. 'He can't talk very well at the moment, of course.'

Somehow, Prince William's birthday prompted his father to drop all sorts of hints about increasing the size of his family. While we now know that it would be more than six months before Diana was again to become pregnant, the Canadians felt as privileged to be the receivers of a whole succession of nod-and-wink signals as Diana was plainly abashed by his continual references in public to something she seemed to regard as rather personal. In Bridgewater, for instance, Charles only just managed to check himself in time when, promising future royal visits to Canada, he declared himself 'sure that we shall be able to send our son - or perhaps several by then (laughter, applause) - and that's not a hint, I assure you!' At a youth festival in Newfoundland the Prince actually expressed a wish for more children, at which Diana blushed and, in her discomfiture, muttered, 'How embarrassing!' He had done a similar thing in public while the couple were in Alberta. 'In private,' Alberta's Premier Brian Peckford explained, 'Diana

The historic visit of the Prince and Princess of Wales to British Columbia, for the opening of *Expo 86* in Vancouver in May 1986. LEFT: Princess Diana meeting children during the first day of the royal visit, in Victoria. ABOVE: Diana waves to quayside admirers as the ferry-boat *Queen of the North* leaves Nanaimo for a leisurely cruise to Vancouver. OPPOSITE PAGE, TOP: the royal couple at Canada Place, site of *Expo 86*, the huge international exhibition of transport and communications technology. BOTTOM: Diana meets a group of women from the Musqeam Indian tribe after the opening ceremonies at *Expo 86*. There was, it seems, general agreement about the use of headbands!

would have come straight back with a quip. But when there's a crowd, she can't do that and she gets embarrassed.'

At the same time, there was no doubting that as a team, Charles and Diana accomplished everything that anyone could reasonably want from them. Their little jokes at each other's expense, which had given a popular gloss to their duties in Australasia, had the Canadians in their turn chuckling with appreciation at the sheer informality of it all. 'Hasn't she got a lovely view from the back?' Prince Charles asked the crowd in Ottawa as he turned to see Diana plunging into yet another group of people on the opposite side of the road. Diana gave back as good as she got. 'It's nearly as old as my husband,' she hooted when somebody showed her a Union Jack that had been made at the time of Queen Victoria's Diamond Jubilee in 1897.

But more importantly, Diana had, by the end of the tour, received a great deal of schooling from her husband. He grew accustomed to admitting his own secondary importance as the roadshow progressed, and contented himself with keeping a watchful, careful eye on his wife, ensuring that she was not being hopelessly swamped, reassuring her by an occasional squeeze of the hand or a brief word snatched in between official ceremonies, or guiding her from one place to another with a deftness of hand that was seen only by the most acute observers.

Moreover, it was obvious that Diana had observed the skills of her husband when it came to the art of exchanging friendly banter with the crowds without uncomfortable pauses, personal familiarity or controversial blunders. 'I've matured a lot recently,' she was confident enough to tell Premier Peckford. 'I've learned a lot, and am doing my job better now than I was before. I'm still finding it very difficult to cope with pressure, but I am learning to cope with it.' In that light, it becomes clear that her very first tour of Canada had rounded off her royal apprenticeship, and it is difficult not to draw comparisons with the result of the 1939 tour on King George and Queen Elizabeth. If, in the Queen's words, that tour 'made us', it must be similarly obvious that the 1983 tour 'made' Diana, and

OPPOSITE PAGE, TOP: Prince Charles and Princess Diana meet children representing various ethnic communities during a civic reception at City Park, Kelowna. BOTTOM LEFT: meeting the stars at a star-studded gala pop concert at the *Expo 86* Theatre in Vancouver. She herself proved something of a star as universal admiration surrounded her stylish and rather unconventional choice of clothes for the occasion. BOTTOM RIGHT: Princess in blue. Diana in the streets of Prince George, where a civic reception awaited her and Prince Charles at the City Hall. THIS PAGE: the Prince and Princess touring part of *Expo 86* early in the afternoon of 6th May. Later in the day, Diana suffered her well-publicised fainting fit – an event that set off rumours of pregnancy.

helped forge her into the self-confident and much more outgoing royal personality she is today.

Three years later, Charles and Diana's next, and much more brief, visit to Canada was concentrated in Vancouver, where the couple opened *Expo 86*. The early part of the visit - a fairly leisurely couple of days in which the royal couple met the Chief of the Nanaimo Indians, some rather younger Indian 'braves' at Kelowna, and enjoyed a river cruise aboard the ferry *Queen of the North* for their journey to Vancouver - was also marred by a volley of criticism of Diana's *déjà-vu* fashions. Fashion-writers throughout British Columbia and beyond seemed to be taking exception to her wearing clothes that had already been seen many times before, and accusing her of the preposterous crime of not being able - or refusing - to afford new clothes.

Fortunately, she had already decided that, for the official opening of *Expo 86* she would wear a stunning black-and-white outfit consisting of a dramatically waisted and flared white jacket over a slim, short, black skirt - all topped by a simple black headband. She followed this up at the *Expo 86* Theatre the next day with a stylish single-breasted black wool dinner jacket and jodhpur-style slacks, over a white silk dress shirt with outsize ruffles down the front. The occasion was a star-studded pop concert, and the Princess' fashion note not only drew whistles, cheers and applause as she arrived at the theatre, but also put paid to the carping that had dogged her since her arrival in the province.

One of the stars at the pop concert was the international rock singer, Bryan Adams, whose then current album featured a song entitled *Diana*, the lyrics of which - *I know he ain't right for you.... Diana, can't you see you drive me wild?.... If you came and lived with me.... Why don't you leave it all behind?....*

- bore rather too close a resemblance to what many saw as a slight on Prince Charles and a poor reflection on the state of the royal marriage. Tactfully, Adams did not perform the song during the show - 'I didn't want to put Prince Charles on the spot,' he explained - and he was duly entranced by the Princess when she met him after the show. 'I'm her greatest fan,' he said. 'She's got lovely style and lovely eyes.'

The monumental and spectacularly presented *Expo 86*, to which the whole world had been invited when the Queen was here in 1983, offered some fascinating insights into transport and communications technology for the royal visitors, and it was a perverse turn of fate that the visit was more memorable for the fact that Diana had the bad luck to experience a fainting fit in full view of the public than for anything else. The incident, which occurred while the Prince and Princess were touring the Californian Pavilion, looked more dramatic than it was, involving as it did a sudden flurry of activity among the security escort and the rather unceremonious bundling of the Princess into a doorway and out of sight. But later, it was confirmed that Diana had suffered nothing more than a brief dizzy spell in the heat of the afternoon, and she did indeed appear happy and fit after a brief rest, waving to well-wishers as she made her way, unaided, back to her car. Understandably enough, the incident resurrected speculation that Diana was again pregnant, but any hopes for news of a third addition to the Wales family in 1986 were quickly squashed by an official assurance from the royal couple's travelling press officer.

But by then, of course, other royal developments were afoot, and this time it was Prince Andrew, and *his* intended, who were at the centre of Canada's attentions.

Prince Edward undertook his first solo trip to Canada in June 1987, spending a week in Nova Scotia as international trustee of the Duke of Edinburgh Award Scheme. OPPOSITE PAGE: the Prince visiting the Halifax Citadel National Historic Park, and walking between a guard of honour found by the troops of the 78th Highlanders. RIGHT: the royal visitor on board *Bluenose*, a replica of a schooner originally launched in 1921, now used to 'fly the flag' for Canada around the world. BELOW: Prince Edward talking with a student at a loom at the Nova Scotia College of Art and Design. BELOW RIGHT: with the Premier of Nova Scotia, John Buchanan, at an official dinner at the World Trade Centre.

'FABULOUS FERGIE': THE YORKS FIND A SECOND HOME

Prince Andrew visited Canada for the last time as a bachelor in 1985. That June, he flew in to Fredericton Airport, New Brunswick for an eight-day stay, the main purpose of which centred on the Canadian Games. Officially, at least, that was the case. But for most of the thousands of young ladies who rose early each day to be at the front of the walkabout crowds, a much more relevant reason for the tour was encapsulated in one admirer's desperate scream: 'Come on, Randy Andy, give us a kiss!' She thrust a rose into his hand to press home her request, but the Prince, no doubt aware that he was one of the world's most eligible bachelors, was adamant. 'If I give you a kiss,' he explained, 'all hell will break loose!' Most people assumed he was referring to the possible reaction among the crowd, but he could equally well have been thinking of the likely effect of such a favour back in England, for only the previous week had his eyes met those of a certain Miss Sarah Ferguson during a lunch party given by the Queen at Windsor Castle during Ascot Week. Unaware of this recent development, however, and thus quite undeterred, the same female admirer approached him further along his route and asked him, 'What do I have to do for a kiss?' Prince Andrew wasn't telling: he merely put on his look of mock surprise and said, 'Oh no; not you again!'

OPPOSITE PAGE: a maple leaf pinned to Sarah's bow provides a popular start to the Yorks' first visit to Canada together in 1987. BELOW: a confident Duchess watches the proceedings in the centre of Toronto. LEFT: Andrew and Sarah become royal tourists at the observation point overlooking Niagara Falls.

But he was willing to get close to the official mascot of the Canadian Games at Saint John - a walking, talking, furry representation of a curled bud of fern, that rejoiced in the name of Fiddlehead. He also got rather too close to a bouquet of flowers that one schoolgirl thrust so firmly towards him that it almost engulfed his face. At Sussex, New Brunswick's Premier Hatfield, clearly forgiven for his rather unfortunate performance before the Prince and Princess of Wales two years earlier, treated Prince Andrew to a barbecue. The royal visitor was also shown the traditional art of horse-shoe throwing, and inspected a prize herd of Jersey cows during a livestock show.

In March of the next year, Prince Andrew and Sarah Ferguson became engaged, and right up to and beyond their gloriously ceremonial wedding in London the following July, it was clear that the example of naturalness and studied informality set by Diana five years earlier was going to become the standard for new, young recruits to the ranks of the Royal Family. This was good news for the Canadians who, while they love their pomp and circumstance as much as anybody, are happier in a more casual vein, know where to draw the line, and thus are able to respond to guests who know likewise.

So it was with the greatest anticipation that Canada prepared to welcome to her shores in the summer of 1987 the first Duke and Duchess of York to visit the country for eighty-

RIGHT: the Duke and Duchess on board *Maid of the Mist* for a journey to the Falls 'curtain'. BELOW: paddling their own canoe on their way to Thunder Bay. OPPOSITE PAGE, TOP: a chic Sarah follows in the steps of a former Duchess of York at Woodbine Racetrack. BOTTOM: respectably hatted for a rodeo at Medicine Hat.

six years. It was their first trip together to any Commonwealth country, and an appropriate choice, too, since for Prince Andrew, it was another return to the country he knows and loves. Indeed, when they arrived in Toronto, he was fulsome in his praise for the surprising transformation the city had undergone since he was last there in 1977. 'I remember the city some years ago not nearly as vibrant and progressive as it is today' he said, 'and that is a great credit to the city and to the people who live in it.' And the Torontonians were pleased to have the Prince and his wife - she who diplomatically sported a red maple leaf below the back of her hat - amongst them. The Yorks were accommodated twenty floors up at the Royal York Hotel, once the most dominant building in the city, but now dwarfed by commercial skyscrapers, and were reminded that the association with York went back a full two centuries - to 1787, when Toronto was called York. The people of Toronto turned out in their thousands in Queen's Park to greet them, providing the biggest crowds the Yorks had seen since their wedding a year earlier, and the royal walkabout route in Nathan Phillips Square was punctuated by hovering clusters of red, white and blue balloons, while the Duke was festooned with a vivid vermilion and saffron garland by a group of Oriental girls in the crowd. Of course, the mood was just right for the Duchess, who climbed up on barrier pedestals to see more of the crowd, offered jokingly to swim across a pool to meet people on the other side of it, posed endlessly for photographs taken by well-wishers who insisted on placing her in position with all the precision of professional photographers, and was enlisted by a small group of female fans in fetching her husband back from further up the walkabout line to meet them.

'It's an unabashed love-in for Fabulous Fergie,' trumpeted one city magazine - but for the visitors, it all seemed too much at times. They didn't appear to know quite which way to go

157

on one of their walkabouts, each floating independently from one side of the route to the other with arms pointing questioningly all over the place, until an escort gave them directions. The Duchess got lost in a crowd of children; the Duke became confused when he suddenly saw what he thought was his own wife in the crowd, then realised it was one of many Fergie lookalikes roaming the Toronto streets; and at a concert at Ontario Place, the royal couple inadvertently kept everyone standing because they had not appreciated that they were expected to be the first to take their seats. Then, to cap it all, the Duke fired a starting pistol to begin a race at the Disabled Olympics, and a piece of wadding flew up into his wife's face. She quickly recovered amid all the consternation sufficiently so, at least, to deliver him a playful punch on the shoulder in revenge. And, as the Prince said at a dinner that evening given by the Canadian government, it's impossible to get it right for everybody. 'Cars are made for people to sit in side by side,' he explained patiently, 'and unfortunately, because everyone has come to see Sarah, I'm on the wrong side all the time!'

Thunder Bay proved an adventure of a different kind. This west Ontario port is impressive enough for any visitor, with its score of grain silos - one of which, holding ten million bushels, is the world's biggest - but to approach it by canoe, as part of a convoy mimicking the voyages of eighteenth-century fur-traders from Montreal, is quite an experience. As, indeed, the Duke and Duchess discovered when they paddled their own fibreglass replicas of the original birch-bark canoes (the Duchess, hilariously, wearing white gloves as if on her way to a Buckingham Palace garden party) towards the shores of Fort William. Here they inspected the fascinating re-creation of life two centuries ago, complete with authentic period costumes and old colonial methods of working. They also came to know how the bay acquired its name, as thunder rolled in from the lake, the heavens opened and a freak storm delivered massive hailstones onto the heads of those not fleet enough of foot to find shelter. And when that was over, the royal couple, under black umbrellas, emerged to visit the canoe sheds, and be presented with the beautifully painted paddles with which

Like the Princess of Wales and Princess Margaret before her, the Duchess of York dressed up to the nines for Edmonton's Klondike Days celebrations. Here LEFT she chats with Prince Andrew on 1885 Street. BELOW LEFT: the Duke and Duchess accepting gifts during their visit to Yellowknife. BELOW: a rather more impressive offering, as Sarah takes charge of a buffalo head presented to the royal couple as a souvenir from Head-Smashed-In-Buffalo-Jump. OPPOSITE PAGE: the casual approach as the Duke and Duchess, fully kitted out, prepare to go down a goldmine at Yellowknife.

they had so gamely propelled themselves into this delightful community earlier. These, it was explained to them, would serve as splendid souvenirs of an absorbing day, and might also come in useful during the canoeing holiday they were scheduled to spend in the Northwest Territories after the official part of the tour was over. For this purpose the visitors were also given a pair of camp stools to help make outdoor life in the Land of the Midnight Sun just a little less uncomfortable.

From Thunder Bay, the Yorks, knowing that no visit to Canada is complete without a trip to Niagara Falls, made for this phenomenal wonder of the world. It took two attempts, since the first helicopter in which they flew developed a fault which its gauge indicator identified as an overheating engine. The craft made a precautionary landing, and the royal party transferred to a second helicopter for the remainder of the journey. They landed close to Table Rock, where they saw their first breathtaking view of the Horseshoe Falls - and, like

millions of tourists before and no doubt after them, neither the Duke nor the Duchess could wait to get their hands on their cameras. The view was even better from top of the nearby tower - so good, in fact, that neither of them took very much notice of the lengthy address that the local dignitaries delivered in their honour, each preferring by far to gaze on the panoramic sights way below the observation windows. The couple then put on bright blue oilskins for one of the most exciting journeys either of them may ever make - a boat trip right up to the edge of the curtain of water that is the Falls. For a time, they were lost to view behind the clouds of mist, and when ultimately they emerged again, the Duchess was busy shaking the moisture out of her spray-drenched hair.

All the makings of Ladies' Day at Royal Ascot awaited the Duke and Duchess the following day as they bowled round Woodbine racecourse at a spanking pace in a gleaming, lacquered landau - Prince Andrew in top-hat and tails, his

No visit to Canada by a young royal couple is really complete without a taste of the great outdoors, and the official end of the 1987 tour was duly followed by a week's holiday during which the Yorks were responsible for propelling themselves along some 300 miles of the Thelon River in the Northwest Territories. In such terrain, it is said, the hardships of everyday life pale into insignificance. Here are blackflies as you've never seen them, and the Duchess wore a protective hood to keep them away. She also wore good, stout hiking boots and a racoon-tailed hat, while Prince Andrew, who, having done all this before and become 'Almost Famous' for it RIGHT, opted for rather more comfortable gear. And this OPPOSITE PAGE, BOTTOM was how they posed for photographers on the morning of their departure, with canoes ready laden and ready for the full royal treatment OPPOSITE PAGE, TOP.

wife in the softest and most feminine of day-dresses and a light hat with sweeping brim that reminded many of that other enthusiastic Woodbine racegoer, the Queen Mother. This, the oldest sporting event in the Canadian calendar, was the 128th running of the Queen's Plate, and it was almost half a century since the first royal visit there.

Between Woodbine and Winnipeg, the royal visitors took a couple of days' rest at a cottage by a lake, where they practised their skills at water-skiing, and came out of the experience, as Prince Andrew put it, 'with our arms stretched out here.' Perhaps that wasn't such a bad thing, for at Winnipeg they had a lot of hand-waving to do, and the Duchess had to stretch enormous distances to claim all the bouquets handed to her from the crowds. One single rose hardly survived the journey from the back of a particularly large crowd, and arrived in her hand wilting and broken. She promptly gave the rest of her flowers to a lady-in-waiting, nipped the two pieces of the rose together with one hand, supported the head with the other, and triumphantly held it aloft for its donor to see. Naturally, she got a big cheer for that!

OPPOSITE PAGE, TOP RIGHT: the Queen Mother's 1987 visit to Montreal began with an inspection of a Black Watch guard of honour. TOP LEFT: after a regimental church service at SS Andrew and Paul Church. BOTTOM: watching the march past at the saluting base in the Percival Molson Memorial Stadium. BELOW: mutual admiration during a Montreal walkabout.

'We're in the party mood,' said Prince Andrew at Edmonton that day, 'and I hope it will continue for the next few days.' The reason? No less than the fact that, as he was reminded that afternoon by the Lieutenant Governor, the royal visitors' first wedding anniversary had, at least according to London time, begun. So, of course, the band struck up the *Anniversary Waltz*, presents were in order, and in true, traditional Canadian style, the two of them were given a fur jacket each. The Duke accepted his (South American-made) version with customary royal reserve; but his wife, more obviously impressed by her massive fox fur, tried it on for size, and enveloped herself in its sheer, luxuriant warmth. The party continued that night with a repeat performance of the royally attended Klondike Days. If the Princess of Wales' act in 1983 seemed hard to follow, the Duchess of York wasn't letting on. She appeared dressed from head to foot in bright blue, her tight-fitting dress edged with abundant frills and her wide-brimmed hat swathed in blue and white ostrich feathers. Hardly, she may have thought, the appropriate dress for travelling in a Victorian wagon down 1885 Street, but that's the way they do it in Edmonton.

There were different dress requirements at Medicine Hat the following day, and this time Prince Andrew was found wanting. Turning up at a Stampede in a lounge suit is no way to behave, and the combination of his grey two-piece and the feathered stetson he was given at the gate was too ridiculous for words. So they loaned him a real cowboy jacket for the occasion instead. The Duchess was altogether better prepared, sporting a bright green buckskin jacket, finely fringed, and

1987. A welcome return to Quebec for the Queen after twenty-five years. OPPOSITE PAGE: an historic arrival signals a renewed relationship. ABOVE: a relaxed walk among the people of Riviere du Loup in the fall sunshine.

looking just the part. This time, the transport really did look out of character, the two rustic-looking visitors being driven to the arena in a beautiful black carriage that would not have looked out of place a few days earlier at Woodbine. But everyone enjoyed the entertainment, which included bull-riding, saddle-bronk riding, steer wrestling and bareback skills, all taken on by people who risked their lives this way because they were, in the words of one of them, 'too lazy to work; too nervous to steal.'

From Medicine Hat, the Duke and Duchess travelled a few miles west to where the great plains meet the Rockies, and to the world heritage site of Head-Smashed-In-Buffalo-Jump. This oddly, though accurately, named location boasts a proven human history as far back as most, as the place where, over the course of some six thousand years, Indians stalked and stampeded some 60 million buffalo to their deaths. Prince Andrew placed its history into perspective by referring to the celebrations that had just taken place that day to mark his own first wedding anniversary, and then comparing this one year of personal history with the millenia of human history that he had come to savour. The couple were here to open a new $20 million, five-storey interpretation centre on the site, in front of robed and feathered representatives of all the Canadian Indian tribes and amid their many rituals and ceremonies. And within the building they saw how generations of buffalo were herded over the cliffs on which the royal party now stood, and onto the plains below where, even now, the bones and skulls lie thirty feet deep. It was a sobering, rivetting experience, yet the organisers had a quite momentous surprise for their visitors. Before leaving, the Duke and Duchess were presented with a massive buffalo head weighing no less than 60 pounds. Taken from an 1,100-lb bull slaughtered the previous year to provide meat for the local tribe, the head had been stuffed and made fit for any wall of Buckingham Palace large enough for the royal couple to choose as a display site. It may say a lot for the Yorks' relationship that it was Sarah who held the gift while Andrew tamely held her bouquet, but even she confessed that she had no idea where she was going to put it.

On this spectacular note, the first York tour of modern times ended, and this young entertaining and entertained couple made ready for the mosquitoes and black-fly of the Northwest Territories where their holiday was to be spent. In Toronto, the Duke had been warned about allowing the press anywhere near them during this stage of the journey. 'Pictures are marvellous things,' he was told, 'providing they do not show your wife disappearing over the end of a canoe and suddenly caught up in the white water.'

So, after the obligatory press-call, the royal party went on its carefree way unaccompanied. In the meantime they could reflect on the fact that the tour had begun with Prince Andrew saying, 'Today sees a new beginning in my Canadian relationship. From now on, it will be ours, and not just mine. This city ten years ago was my second home: I hope that it will continue to be not just mine, but *our* second home in Canada.'

It had finished with equally touching words from both of them. At a farewell dinner at Edmonton, the Duke told his audience that the new chapter he had spoken of in Toronto had 'turned out to be a whole new volume, and in which Sarah features in every page.' For her part, Sarah put it just as movingly: 'Thank you, Albertans, and all Canadians, for looking after us so well and for such an amazing introduction to my first tour. You make us feel so at home here. *Au revoir*; *à bientôt*: they both sound less final than Goodbye.'

In those simple words is the essence of the relationship between the Crown and the nation of Canada over the years:

the knowledge on the part of both the Royal Family and Canadians generally that there will always be another time, another opportunity to enjoy celebrations together, to experience the mutual fascination of each other's company, to admire what each has to offer the other. And, above all, to confirm and strengthen a unique friendship that has grown and been nurtured by two centuries of increasing familiarity and understanding. King George V may well have impressed himself and others by recording the number of hands he shook while in Canada in 1901; there is a certain grandiosity in the monumental figures that indicate the extent of any particular tour's significance - the plaques unveiled, the trees planted, the toasts proposed, the anthems played, the visitors' books signed, the speeches made and listened to, the bouquets received. But, as the Duke of Edinburgh made clear after his first Canadian experience, way back in 1951, 'I am not greatly impressed by statistics, and it does not matter how many miles we went by train, by air or by car. What is important is that we made personal contact.'

OPPOSITE PAGE, TOP: tight security in Quebec despite a warm, and somewhat curious, reception BOTTOM from the people of the capital. BELOW: the Queen insists on inspecting the Vingt-Deux despite the snow. OVERLEAF: within sight of her 89th birthday, the Queen Mother in Toronto fifty years after her first visit with King George VI.

ROYAL VISITS TO CANADA YEAR BY YEAR
1786-1989

This quick-reference summary lists all the State, major official, and most of the semi-official visits made to Canada by members of the Royal Family to date, along with the periods of residence of royal Governors General, and some of the more notable informal excursions undertaken by royalty in a purely or mainly private capacity.

1786-87	Prince William, the future King William IV, came to Canada as part of a naval contingent serving in North America and the West Indies.
1791-98, 1799-1800	Prince Edward, fourth son of King George III, stayed in Canada on military duties and as Commander of British North American troops.
1860	Albert Edward, Prince of Wales, undertook a two-month tour of Upper and Lower Canada.
1861	Prince Alfred spent five weeks in the Maritime Provinces, Newfoundland and Lower Canada.
1869-70	Prince Arthur spent a year in Canada with the Rifle Brigade based at Montreal.
1878-83	The Marquess of Lorne, accompanied by his wife, Princess Louise, resided in Canada as Governor-General. Many members of the Royal Family visited them during this time.
1890	The Duke of Connaught, formerly Prince Arthur, toured Canada for several weeks.
1900	Princess Marie-Louise cut short an intended holiday in Canada, at the insistence of her husband, Prince Aribert of Anhalt, and of Queen Victoria.
1901	The Duke and Duchess of Cornwall and York toured Canada coast-to-coast as part of an Empire-wide voyage.
1906	Prince Arthur of Connaught spent several weeks touring Canada.
1908	George, Prince of Wales, visited Quebec for the city's tercentenary.
1911-16	The Duke of Connaught, accompanied by the Duchess of Connaught and Princess Patricia, resided in Canada as Governor-General.
1913	Prince Albert, the future King George VI, visited parts of

	Canada during his service with the Royal Navy, with his ship, HMS *Cumberland*.
1919	Edward, Prince of Wales, undertook a two-month tour of Canada.
1923	Edward, Prince of Wales, visited his ranch in Alberta, calling in at many major towns and cities over a seven-week period.
1924	Edward, Prince of Wales, paid another visit to his ranch, as part of an unofficial tour of Canada.
1926	Prince George visited parts of Canada, including the West coast.
1927	Edward, Prince of Wales, and Prince George visited Canada for the Diamond Jubilee of the Confederation.
1928	Prince George paid a private visit to Canada.
1929	Prince Henry spent a short time privately in Canada.
1939	King George VI and Queen Elizabeth undertook a six-week coast-to-coast tour of Canada.
1940-46	The Earl of Athlone, with his wife Princess Alice, resided in Canada as Governor-General.
1941	The Duke of Kent (formerly Prince George) visited air bases and training centres in Canada.
1941	The Duke and Duchess of Windsor visited their ranch near Calgary.
1945	Viscount Lascelles (now Earl of Harewood) joined the staff of Government House as A.D.C. to the Earl of Athlone.
1945	The Duke and Duchess of Windsor spent a short holiday in New Brunswick.
1951	Princess Elizabeth and the Duke of Edinburgh undertook a coast-to-coast tour of Canada.
1954	
July/August	The Duke of Edinburgh undertook a three-week tour of Canada, during which he visited the British Empire Games at Vancouver, travelled in the Yukon, and visited an Inuit settlement within the Arctic Circle.
August/September	The Duchess of Kent and Princess Alexandra paid a two-week visit touring Quebec and Ontario.
November	The Queen Mother paid a five-day visit to Ottawa.
1955	
November	Mary, Princess Royal, visited six Canadian cities.
1957	
October	The Queen and Duke of Edinburgh visited to open the 23rd Canadian Parliament.
1958	
July	Princess Margaret toured British Columbia to celebrate the province's centenary, and visited other parts of Canada.
October	Prince Philip visited to preside at two meetings during the world conference at Ottawa of the English-Speaking Union of the Commonwealth.
1959	
June/July	The Queen and Prince Philip toured for six weeks, during which the Queen opened the new St Lawrence Seaway, and visited many outlying districts never before seen by a reigning monarch.

1960

June · Prince Philip visited Ottawa and Toronto in connection with the Second Commonwealth Study Conference to be held in Canada in 1962.

1962

May · Prince Philip visited Montreal to open the Second Commonwealth Study Conference.

June · The Queen Mother visited Montreal for the centenary celebration of the Black Watch (Royal Highland Regiment) of Canada, of which she is Colonel-in-Chief.

June · Mary, Princess Royal, visited Vancouver, Toronto, Ottawa and Kingston.

1964

August/September · Prince William of Gloucester paid a private visit to Ontario, Manitoba, Saskatchewan and British Columbia.

October · The Queen and Prince Philip visited for centennial celebrations commemorating visits of the Fathers of Confederation to Charlottetown and Quebec City.

1965

June · The Queen Mother visited in connection with the jubilee celebrations of the Toronto Scottish Regiment.

1966

March · Prince Philip visited Toronto and Ottawa.

1967

May/June · Princess Alexandra undertook a three-week tour of seven provinces.

June · State Visit by the Queen and Prince Philip for the 100th anniversary of Confederation, and to visit *Expo 67* in Montreal.

June · Princess Margaret and Lord Snowdon visited *Expo 67* in Montreal, and went on to Toronto.

July · Prince Philip visited to open the Pan-American Games.

July · The Queen Mother toured the Atlantic Provinces for two weeks, visiting New Brunswick, Nova Scotia, Prince Edward Island and Newfoundland.

October · Princess Alexandra attended British Week in Toronto.

November · Prince Philip opened the Royal Agricultural Winter Fair and attended the conference of the Royal Agricultural Society of the Commonwealth in Toronto.

1968

June · The Duke and Duchess of Kent visited Calgary to open the Stampede and Exhibition.

1969

October/November · Prince Philip visited in connection with the Duke of Edinburgh Award Scheme.

1970

July · The Prince of Wales undertook a two-day visit to Ottawa.

July · The Queen, Prince Philip, Prince of Wales and Princess Anne visited to mark the centenaries of Northwest Territories and Manitoba.

1971

May · The Queen and Prince Philip, with Princess Anne, attended the centennial celebrations of the province of British Columbia.

| September | Princess Margaret and Lord Snowdon visited to open a new art gallery in Winnipeg. |

1973

February	Prince Michael of Kent visited the World Bobsleigh Championships in Montreal.
June	Princess Alexandra visited Nova Scotia.
July	The Queen and Prince Philip visited Ontario, Prince Edward Island, Saskatchewan and Alberta.
July/August	The Queen and Prince Philip visited Ottawa to attend the meeting of the Commonwealth heads of Government.

1974

January	Princess Anne paid an official visit to Ottawa with Captain Mark Phillips.
April	Prince Michael of Kent visited Ottawa with the British Ministry of Defence.
May	Princess Margaret visited to celebrate Winnipeg's centenary.
June	The Queen Mother paid a week's visit in connection with the presentation of new Colours to the Toronto Scottish Regiment in Toronto, and to the Black Watch (Royal Highland Regiment) of Canada in Montreal.
November	Princess Anne visited the Royal Agricultural Winter Fair in Toronto, with Captain Mark Phillips.

1975

| April | The Prince of Wales served in HMS *Hermes* in Canadian waters for three weeks and, besides a three-day visit to Ottawa, spent a week in the Northwest Territories. |
| June | The Duke and Duchess of Kent visited Toronto as guests of the Ontario Jockey Club for the running of the Queen's Plate. |

1976

| July | The Queen and Prince Philip toured Nova Scotia and New Brunswick before opening and attending the Olympic Games in Montreal, accompanied by Prince Andrew and, briefly, the Prince of Wales and Prince Edward. Princess Anne competed with the British team in the equestrian event, and Captain Mark Phillips was also present. |

1977

January-July	Prince Andrew attended Lakefield College School, Ontario for two terms.
July	The Prince of Wales visited Alberta to take part in the celebrations marking the centennial of the signing of Treaty No. 7 by the Blackfoot, Blood, Peigan, Sarcee and Stony Indian tribes, ceding the prairies of southern Alberta to the British Crown.
October	The Queen and Prince Philip visited Ottawa as part of the Queen's Silver Jubilee celebrations.
November/December	Prince Philip visited Regina for meetings of the Royal Agricultural Society of the Commonwealth.

1978

| February | Prince Philip attended the preliminary planning meetings at Toronto for the 1980 Commonwealth Study Conference. |
| July/August | The Queen and Prince Philip toured Canada, visiting Newfoundland, Saskatchewan and Alberta, and, with Prince Andrew, attending the Eleventh Commonwealth Games. |

August	Prince Philip returned to Canada to close the Commonwealth Games.
October	Prince Philip received the St Boniface General Hospital Research Foundation's Annual Award for 1978 at Winnipeg.

1979

April	The Prince of Wales, during an official visit to Canada, combined other official Canadian engagements with his first visit to Pearson College in his capacity as President of the International Council of the United World Colleges.
May	The Duke of Kent visited the Lorne Scots at Brampton.
June/July	The Queen Mother paid a week-long visit to Halifax, Nova Scotia, and Toronto.
September	Prince and Princess Michael of Kent visited Toronto.
October	Prince Philip visited to attend meetings in connection with the Duke of Edinburgh's Fifth Commonwealth Study Conference.
November	Princess Anne visited Ottawa and Ontario in connection with the Save the Children Fund.

1980

March/April	The Prince of Wales visited Ottawa and British Columbia as President of the International Council of United World Colleges.
April/May	Princess Alexandra visited Toronto, Nanaimo and Victoria.
May	Prince Philip visited to attend the Duke of Edinburgh's Fifth Commonwealth Study Conference in Ontario and Quebec.
July	Princess Margaret visited Saskatchewan and Alberta to attend centenary celebrations.
August	Prince and Princess Michael of Kent visited Montreal.
September/October	Prince Philip visited Canada as part of a tour of North America.

1981

July	The Queen Mother visited Ontario to attend the bicentennial celebrations at Niagara-on-the-Lake, and to visit regiments of which she is Colonel-in-Chief.
July	Princess Margaret and Lady Sarah Armstrong-Jones visited Ontario in connection with the fiftieth anniversary celebrations of the Royal Ballet.

1982

April	The Queen and Prince Philip visited Canada for the Patriation Ceremony in Ottawa.
July	Princess Anne visited Yukon, Saskatchewan, Manitoba and Ottawa.
October	The Prince of Wales visited the Lester B Pearson College of the Pacific in British Columbia.

1983

March	The Queen and Prince Philip paid a brief visit to British Columbia.
June	The Duke of Gloucester visited Ottawa to attend, as Grand Prior, the centenary of the foundation of the Priory of Canada of the Venerable Order of St John.
June	The Prince and Princess of Wales undertook a 17-day tour of the Maritime Provinces, Ottawa and Alberta.
June/July	Prince Philip visited for the centenary of the Royal Canadian Regiment.

July/August	Prince Andrew spent a three-week private visit in the Northwest Territories.
October	The Duke of Kent visited Toronto as Colonel-in-Chief of the Lorne Scots Regiment.

1984

February	Prince Michael of Kent visited Nova Scotia in connection with the 75th anniversary celebrations of the first powered flight in the British Empire.
July	Prince Philip visited New Brunswick to present new Colours to the 2nd Battalion, Royal Canadian Regiment.
September/October	The Queen visited New Brunswick and Ontario with Prince Philip, and went on to Manitoba alone.

1985

June	Prince Philip visited in connection with the Duke of Edinburgh Award Scheme.
June/July	Prince Andrew made his first official solo visit to Canada, touring New Brunswick, Nova Scotia and Ontario.
June	The Queen Mother spent a week visiting Toronto and Saskatchewan.
August	Prince Philip carried out a three-day visit to Alberta.
November	Princess Alexandra visited Toronto and Ottawa.

1986

April/May	The Prince and Princess of Wales visited British Columbia and opened *Expo 86* in Vancouver.
June	Princess Anne visited Alberta, Ontario and New Brunswick.
July	Princess Margaret visited Vancouver for five days in connection with *Expo 86*.

1987

June	Prince Philip visited in connection with the World Wide Fund for Nature and the Duke of Edinburgh Award Scheme.
June	The Queen Mother visited Montreal to celebrate the 125th anniversary of the Black Watch (Royal Highland Regiment) of Canada.
June	Prince Edward spent a week in Canada, mainly in Nova Scotia.
July	The Duke and Duchess of York visited Ontario, Manitoba, Alberta and Northwest Territories; their first official visit to Canada.
October	The Queen and Prince Philip stayed in British Columbia for the Commonwealth heads of Government meeting, and subsequently toured Saskatchewan and Quebec.

1988

February	The Princess Royal visited the Winter Olympic Games in Calgary, Alberta.
June	Princess Margaret visited Nova Scotia and Toronto.

1989

July	The Queen Mother visited Montreal, Toronto and London, Ontario.
July	The Duke and Duchess of York spent two weeks in Canada, undertaking engagements in the provinces of Prince Edward Island, Quebec, Saskatchewan and the National Capital Region.

BIBLIOGRAPHY

The author has consulted the following publications in the course of research for this book:

Books
Anon: *The King to his People* Williams & Norgate (1935)
Anon: *The Royal Family in Wartime* Odhams Press (1945)
Anon: *Their Majesties' Visit To Canada* Macmillan (1939)
Anon: *Charles, Present Prince, Future King* World International Publishing (1981)
Anon ed: *His Majesty's Speeches: The Record of The Silver Jubilee* King George's Jubilee Trust (1935)
Anon: *Princess Diana: A Year of Triumph* Astrian Marketing (1983)
Athlone, Princess Alice, Countess of: *For My Grandchildren* Evans Brothers (1979)
Baker, George: *HRH Prince Philip, Duke of Edinburgh* Cassell (1961)
Benson, Arthur C & Esher, Viscount ed: *The Letters of Queen Victoria, 1837-1861, Volumes I-III*
    John Murray (1908)
Benson, E F: *King Edward VII* Longmans, Green (1933)
Bloch, Michael: *The Duke of Windsor's War* Weidenfeld & Nicolson (1982)
Bolitho, Hector: *King Edward VIII: His Life & Reign* Eyre & Spottiswoode (1938)
Bolitho, Hector: *Their Majesties* Max Parrish (1952)
Boothroyd, Basil: *Philip: An Informal Biography* Longman (1971)
Brooke, John: *King George III* BCA (1972)
Brook-Shepherd, G: *Uncle of Europe* BCA (1975)
Brown, Michele: *Prince Charles: A Biography* Artus (1980)
Brown, Michele: *Prince Charles & Princess Diana* Methuen (1984)
Bryan, J III & Murphy, Charles J V: *The Windsor Story* BCA (1980)
Butler, Peter comp: *The Wit of Prince Philip* Leslie Frewin (1965)
Campbell, Judith: *Elizabeth and Philip* Arthur Barker (1972)
Campbell, Judith: *Charles, A Prince of our Time* Octopus (1981)
Cathcart, Helen: *Her Majesty* W H Allen (1962)
Cathcart, Helen: *The Queen Mother* Mayflower-Dell (1966)
Clark, Stanley: *Palace Diary* Harrap (1958)
Cooke, Alistair: *Six Men* BCA (1977)
Coolican, Don: *Charles, Royal Adventurer* BCA (1978)
Courtney, Nicholas: *Prince Andrew* Macdonald (1983)
Crawford, Marion: *The Queen Mother* George Newnes (1951)
Darbyshire, Taylor: *In the Words of the King* Hutchinson (1938)
Darbyshire, Taylor: *The Duke of York* Hutchinson
Dean, John: *HRH Prince Philip, Duke of Edinburgh* Robert Hale (c1952)
Devon Stanley: *The Royal Canadian Tour* Pitkin (1951)
Donaldson, Frances: *Edward VIII* BCA (1974)
Donaldson, Frances: *King George VI & Queen Elizabeth* Weidenfeld & Nicolson (1977)
Duff, David: *George & Elizabeth* Collins (1983)
Duff, David: *The Life Story of HRH Princess Louise, Duchess of Argyll* Stanley Paul (1940)
Duncan, Andrew: *The Reality of Monarchy* Heinemann (1970)
Edgar, Donald: *Prince Andrew* Arthur Baker (1980)
Eyck, Frank: *The Prince Consort* Cedric Chivers (1975)
Fisher, G & H: *Prince Andrew, Boy, Man & Prince* W H Allen (1981)
Fisher, G & H: *Prince Charles, the Future King* W H Allen (1966)
Frankland, Noble: *Prince Henry, Duke of Gloucester* Weidenfeld & Nicolson (1980)
Fulford, Roger: *The Prince Consort* Macmillan (1949)
Gordon, Keith V: *North America Sees Our King & Queen* Hutchinson (1939)
Gore, John: *King George V – A Personal Memoir* John Murray (1949)
Gray, Robert & Olivier, Jane: *Edward VIII: The Man We Lost* Compton Press (1972)
Hall, Trevor: *In Celebration of the Queen's Visit to Canada* CLB (1984)
Hall, Trevor: *Royal Family Yearbook* CLB (1982)
Hall, Trevor: *The Queen Mother and Her Family* CLB (1983)
Hall, Trevor: *The Story of Prince Andrew* CLB (1983)
Hamilton, Willie MP: *My Queen and I* Quartet Books (1975)
Hibbert, Christopher: *Edward VII – A Portrait* Allen Lane (1977)
Hobhouse, Hermione: *Prince Albert – His Life and Work* Hamish Hamilton (1983)
Holden, Anthony: *Charles, Prince of Wales* BCA (1979)
Holmes, Richard ed: *Edward VII – His Life and Times* Amalgamated Press (1910)
Hussein, Anwar: *HRH Prince Andrew* Hamlyn (1979)

Hussein, Anwar: *HRH Prince Charles* Hamlyn (1978)
Jeffrey, Robert & Russell, Paul: *The Canadian Royal Tour* Methuen (1983)
Judd, Denis: *Prince Philip: A Biography* BCA (1980)
Junor, Penny: *Diana, Princess of Wales* Sidgwick & Jackson (1983)
King, Stella: *Princess Marina: Her Life and Times* Cassell (1969)
Laird, Dorothy: *How The Queen Reigns* Pan (1959)
Laird, Dorothy: *Queen Elizabeth the Queen Mother* Hodder & Stoughton (1966)
Lee, Sir Sidney: *King Edward VII: A Biography* Macmillan (1925 and 1927)
Levenson, David & Hall, Trevor: *Charles and Diana Visit Canada* CLB (1983)
Levenson, David & Hall, Trevor: *The Story of Diana* Collins (1985)
Lindsay Keir, David: *The Constitutional History of Modern Britain* A & C Black (1961)
Liversidge, Douglas: *Prince Charles: Monarch in the Making* Panther (1979)
Liversidge, Douglas: *The Queen Mother* Panther (1979)
Lorne, Marquess of: *VRI – Her Life and Empire* Harmsworth (1901)
Mackenzie, Compton: *The Windsor Tapestry* Rich & Cowan (1938)
Mackenzie, F A: *King George V In His Own Words* Ernest Benn (1929)
Magnus, Philip: *King Edward the Seventh* Penguin (1967)
Maine, Basil: *Our Ambassador King* Hutchinson (1936)
Marie-Louise, Princess: *My Memories of Six Reigns* Penguin (1960)
Maxwell, Herbert: *Sixty Years A Queen* Harmsworth (1897)
Morris, Jan: *Spectacle of Empire* Faber & Faber (1982)
Morton, Andrew: *The Royal Yacht Britannia* Orbis (1984)
Morton, Andrew: *Duchess* Michael O'Mara (1988)
Netherlands, HRH Princess Wilhelmina of: *Lonely But Not Alone* Hutchinson (1960)
Nicolson, Harold: *King George V: His Life and Reign* Constable (1952)
Ollard, Richard ed: *Prince Philip Speaks* Collins (1960)
Philip, HRH Prince: *Selected Speeches: 1948-1955* OUP (1957)
Pope Hennessy, J: *Queen Mary* George Allen & Unwin (1959)
Price, Harry: *The Royal Tour, 1901* Webb & Bower (1980)
Pye, Michael: *The Windsors in Exile* Hamlyn (1982)
Rippon, Angela: *Mark Phillips: The Man and his Horses* David & Charles (1982)
St Aubyn, Giles: *Edward VII: Prince and King* Collins (1979)
St Aubyn, Giles: *William of Gloucester* Muller
Sandres, G Ivy: *Edward, Prince of Wales* Nisbet & Co (1921)
Simmonds, Diana: *Princess Di, The National Dish* Pluto Press (1984)
Wakeford, Geoffrey: *The Heir Apparent* Sphere (1968)
Watson, J Steven: *The Reign of George III 1760-1815* OUP (1963)
Wentworth-Day, J: *HRH Princess Marina, Duchess of Kent* Robert Hale (1962)
Wheeler-Bennett, J: *King George VI* Macmillan (1958)
Windsor, HRH the Duke of: *A King's Story* Cassell (1951)
Woodham-Smith, Cecil: *Queen Victoria – Her Life & Times, 1819-1861* Cardinal/Sphere (1975)
York, Rosemary comp: *Charles In His Own Words* Omnibus Press (1981)
Young, Gordon: *Voyage of State* Hodder & Stoughton (1939)
Yugoslavia, Queen Alexandra of: *Prince Philip* May Fair (1961)
Ziegler, Philip: *King William IV* Fontana (1973)

Periodicals
Canadian Geographical Journal: Royal Visit Number, July 1939
Everybodys: The Princess in Canada, 27 October 1951
Sphere: The Queen in Canada, 19 October 1957
National Geographical Magazine: The Duke of Edinburgh's World Tour, November 1957